MAUREEN FISCHER

RETRO BAKING

100 CLASSIC CONTEST WINNERS UPDATED FOR TODAY

COLLECTORS PRESS

PORTLAND, OREGON

Book Design: Lisa M. Douglass, Collectors Press, Inc.
Editor: Sue Mann
Proofreader: Jade Chan

Library of Congress Cataloging-in-Publication Data

Fischer, Maureen M.
  Retro baking : 100 classic contest winners updated for today / Maureen Fischer.-- 1st American ed.
     p. cm. -- (Retro series)
  Includes index.
  ISBN 1-888054-95-6 (hardcover : alk. paper)
  1. Baking. 2. Desserts. 3. Cookery, American. I. Title. II. Series.
  TX765.F49 2004
  641.8'15--dc22
                              2004013361

Printed in Singapore

9 8 7 6 5 4 3 2 1

Collectors Press books are available at special discounts for bulk purchases, premiums, and promotions. Special editions, including personalized inserts or covers, and corporate logos, can be printed in quantity for special purposes. For further information contact: Special Sales, Collectors Press, Inc., P.O. Box 230986, Portland, OR 97281. Toll free: 1-800-423-1848.

Retro Baking is part of the *Retro* Series by Collectors Press, Inc.

For a free catalog write: Collectors Press, Inc., P. O. Box 230986, Portland, OR 97281. Toll free: 1-800-423-1848 or visit our website at: collectorspress.com.

contents!

Remember thrill-seeking Westerns on the radio and black-and-white TV sets? What about poodle skirts, bobby socks, and 45s on the record player? How about speckled linoleum floors and pastel-colored dishes? It was a simpler time, when Dad was home by six and Mom had a hot, wholesome dinner on the table waiting for the family. All the joy and whimsy of those days are here for you to taste in *Retro Baking*, a recipe collection of baked favorites taken from the recipe contests of yesterday. Made for today's cooks, but stirred with memories, these recipes are time-tested favorites you'll use again and again – we promise!

World War II was behind us and the late 1940s and the 1950s brought a new lease on life. American life had a sense of abundance, and it showed in the kitchens of homes all over the country. Many women who had filled in for absent workers during the war years reclaimed the opportunity to stay home. They devoted their time to the pursuits of homemaking and the care of their families – which, of course, included baking. Nothing was as wonderful as fresh cookies in the cookie jar or a loaf of warm bread served with meatloaf and mashed potatoes. Cakes and pies were showcased at picnics, potlucks, and bake sales. Desserts, glamorous and elegant, were the perfect ending to meals created just for company or family. It was a carefree time, a time to relax and enjoy life!

Families enjoyed more leisure time than ever before, and this extra time paid off as families looked for new ways to entertain family and friends. In the kitchen, cooks gussied up evening family meals or planned elaborate meals, including using their best china, for guests. The backyard or the park, as well as the dining room, became a place to entertain. Picnics and tailgating were popular. Neighbors went to each others' kitchens on weekday mornings and shared cake and coffee during coffee klatches. With Mom often home, she and the kids baked batches of cookies and loaves of bread, or pies for dessert. So baking and cooking was simply not a chore done to sustain the family but a creative activity that allowed cooks to share and enjoy time with others.

With all the creative juices flowing and homemakers having more free time available, it didn't take long for food companies, publishing houses, and even restaurants to tap these resourceful homemakers for their best ideas and recipes. A call for recipes to be entered into contests was certainly not a new idea, but it was one that had great potential. Contestants had a chance to show off their best recipes while being acknowledged for their expertise and ingenuity. And, of course, there was the opportunity to win a wonderful prize! Sometimes prizes included cash, which was always a welcome boon to families, but the real prize was basking in the spotlight and receiving accolades from peers.

Food companies, on the other hand, found using recipe contests a good way to encourage cooks to use their products, to generate new ideas, and to find out more about their consumers. One of the most popular recipe contests, the Pillsbury Bake-Off®, began in 1949 as the "Grand National Recipe and Baking Contest" and was held at the elegant Waldorf-Astoria Hotel in New York City. It was started as a way to celebrate the eightieth birthday of the Pillsbury Company and promised a whopping $50,000 for the grand prize recipe. An invitation went out to all cooks to share their most beloved recipes. The response was overwhelming. One hundred contestants included ninety-seven women and three men who, after being selected from all entrants, prepared their own recipes and presented them to the

judges. Soon after, Pillsbury decided to make it an annual event. The competition was referred to as the Bake-Off Contest®, a name that became the official title of the contest. The Pillsbury Bake-Off® is still held biannually at different locales throughout the country and includes a wide range of contestants: teens, men, retired folks, housewives, and working moms. Judges still select one hundred finalists, but the grand prize has jumped to $1 million.

Although the Pillsbury Bake-Off® was among the most well-known cooking and baking competitions, other food companies also offered contestants the chance to compete for prizes. Recipe contests included competitions using flour, gelatin, fruit, cereals, yeast, refrigerated pie crusts, cornmeal, chocolate, and leavening products. Some competitions asked contestants to submit any favorite recipe; others required only original, unpublished recipes. Participants relied on old-fashioned, American kitchen ingenuity and a can-do attitude to create and enter original ones. Early contests have given us recipes we take for granted today: Peanut Blossoms, Pineapple Upside-Down Cake, and Cherry Winks.

During the postwar boom years convenience foods proliferated. Keeping the tradition of wholesome family meals and that fanciful dessert for company, cooks started to turn to products that made life easier – still homemade but with a little help! In 1939 Nestle Corporation sold the first bag of chocolate chips, and Toll House Cookies became a runaway hit for moms and kids alike. Both Pillsbury and General Mills introduced their first boxed cake mixes to consumers in 1948, ushering in a more convenient way to bake cake.

Cooks also turned to experts for new ideas and inspiration as well as for basic cooking questions. In 1924 the nation's first cooking show, which was broadcast in Minneapolis, was hosted by "Betty Crocker." Later *The Betty Crocker School of the Air* became a national radio show and ran for twenty-four years as it aided homemakers in the kitchen. Food enthusiast James Beard offered the first television cooking show in 1946, educating viewers on how to bake and cook. In 1950 network television premiered the *Kraft Television Theater*. The show, sponsored by Kraft Food Company, used the commercial time for how-to cooking demonstrations. As media and the food industry became more entwined, women's magazines, radio, and finally television became the facilitators for sharing advertisements for everything a homemaker might need, from chocolate to cake mix and from dishwashers to blenders. They also inspired and encouraged cooks to experiment and have confidence in their cooking abilities, taking some to the next level: entering the recipe contest.

Although food companies turned up the heat on cooking competitions, so did commodities like poultry growers. Encouraging cooks to use chicken and concoct new chicken recipes, Maryland hosted the First Annual Chicken Cookoff in 1949 at the Delmarva Chicken Festival, a tristate event with Delaware and Virginia. As the popularity of the contest grew, the National Chicken Council took the reins and premiered the National Chicken Cooking Contest. Contestants and their recipes were selected from each state plus the District of Columbia to compete for top honors. In 1983, with increasing interest and growth, the contest decided to change the competition to a biannual event. In 1974 the cattle industry followed suit, and a group of ranchers' wives formed the National Beef Cook-Off®. Although beef consumption continued to increase in the decades after World War II, beef sales lost their foothold during the 1970s. The contest was a way to jump-start the interest in beef.

Food companies and commodities were not the only ones turning to homemakers in search of creativity. Early turn-of-the-century newspapers viewed recipe contests as a valuable tool for boosting circulation and even for encouraging the use of advertisers' products. Magazines like *Sunset* and *Better Homes and Gardens* followed the trend and formulated their own recipe contests. *Better Homes and Gardens* began an annual recipe contest in 1923 with winners receiving $5 and, of course, the privilege of having their names and recipes featured in the magazine. Later, the contest became a monthly feature, each month offering a different recipe subject. The Prize Tested Recipes® contest is still going strong, and today's top winner from each category collects a cool $400 for the most-prized recipe. At the end of the year, an annual grand prize winner is chosen from all the monthly winners.

At the grassroots level of all recipe contests, you'll find county and state fairs. These gatherings, held since the early 1800s, have been at the forefront of recipe contests. Originally cozy county get-togethers, they were held annually to allow cooks to show off their best local recipes. Larger state fairs included people who cooked, baked, and canned with local ingredients to create their blue-ribbon best. These cooks knew their entries had to endure travel time, often for hundreds of miles, waiting for judging day (with so many entries they could not all be judged on one day), and strict criteria for judging. Those who won the coveted blue ribbons were assured their recipes were the best.

Most cooks have come to associate blue-ribbon recipes as the best of the best. Baking is important in these contests, which are comprised of a huge variety of categories like angel food cake, chiffon cake, bar cookies, Grandma's favorite cookies, fruit pies, pizza, meat pies, rolls, and quick breads. And the list goes on and on. Fair competitors often entered foods in multiple categories. As the popularity of these recipe contests grew, national food companies began to sponsor fair-associated contests, with special prizes for the top winners using their products.

Recipe contests continue to be a popular outlet for creativity, and there are always new recipes to be sampled. Many winning recipes in *Retro Baking* may have been hidden away, tucked in worn recipe boxes as newer recipes replaced them. But these classics are definitely not forgotten. *Retro Baking* revives the tantalizing treats of yesteryear, celebrating and adding a modern twist to make these timeless favorites as popular as they were in their own day.

breads
and
rolls

Bread is known as the staff of life, a staple that accompanies the most humble and the most exquisite meals. Accomplished bread bakers were held in the highest esteem because making good bread was no easy task. They didn't have the luxury of purchased yeast and had to make their own. This "starter" varied in strength from batch to batch, which made working the dough a temperamental process. In the late 1860s, however, compressed yeast cakes were developed. This fresh yeast leavened bread marvelously and consistently, but it had to be refrigerated and had a limited storage life. In the 1940s active dry yeast was invented to ensure that our fighting men had home-baked bread. The yeast gave cooks new flexibility and more predictability in their bread making.

After the turn of the century, packaged whole loaves of bread started appearing on store shelves, easing the rigors of daily or weekly baking.

In the 1920s, sliced bread was introduced to American households, but with the advent of World War II and rationing, the U.S. Secretary of Agriculture banned commercially sliced bread to keep costs down. Once again, cooks began baking their own bread in earnest to save pennies and to keep up the war effort on the home front.

Unlike showy, spectacular food creations, bread is a wholesome, everyday staple woven into our daily lives. Although a loaf of bread may not seem memorable, loaves of speckled wheat bread, white bread, dark pungent rye, and farmhouse favorites like oatmeal bread or buttermilk bread kept families going and growing. Meals were accompanied by baskets of warm Parker House rolls, delicate fan tans, or hearty potato rolls. Fragrant, warm cinnamon-raisin rolls and sticky caramel rolls greeted early-morning risers.

More than just serving bread, it was the creating of bread that mattered. The mixing, kneading, shaping, rising, and baking gave cooks a sense of accomplishment, the house an unforgettable aroma, and family members a sense of eager anticipation.

With all the conveniences of our modern times, we forget the pleasure and the joy of making and enjoying home-made bread. Here are recipes, updated for today's cooks, that honor the old-fashioned, homespun breads Mom (and Grandma) used to make. Just add love.

cheesy bread

1 3/4 cups water
1/2 cup cornmeal, plus additional for sprinkling
2 tsps salt
1/2 cup molasses
2 tbsps shortening
1 pkg active dry yeast
1/2 cup warm water
4 to 5 cups all-purpose flour, sifted
1 pound American cheese

rease and flour two 8-inch round pans and set aside. In medium saucepan combine water, cornmeal, and salt. Stirring constantly, bring to a low boil and cook until slightly thickened. Remove from heat and add molasses and shortening. Cool to lukewarm. In large bowl dissolve yeast in warm water. Thoroughly blend in cornmeal mixture. Gradually add flour until stiff dough is formed. Turn onto well-floured surface and knead approximately 5 minutes or until smooth. Put dough in greased bowl, cover, and place in warm place until doubled, approximately 1 to 1 1/2 hours. Cut cheese into 1/2-inch cubes. Lightly sprinkle work surface with cornmeal and place dough in middle. Place half the cheese cubes on top of dough and work them in. Add remaining cheese cubes and continue to work them in until cheese is evenly distributed. Separate dough in half, shape into round loaves, place in pans; be sure to work in any exposed cheese cubes. Let rise in warm place 1 hour. Bake at 350 degrees 45 to 50 minutes.

golden butter bread

4 1/4 cups all-purpose flour, divided
1/2 cup white sugar
1 tsp salt
2 1/4 tsps active dry yeast
1 cup milk
1/2 cup butter
2 eggs
2 tsps vanilla extract

In large bowl combine 2 cups flour, sugar, salt, and yeast; set aside. In medium saucepan heat milk and butter until just warm. Beat in eggs and vanilla. Add liquid mixture to flour mixture; beat well about 2 minutes. Stir in remaining flour to make medium-stiff batter. Cover, place in warm spot, and let rise 1 hour. Punch down dough and place in greased 10-inch loaf pan. Cover and let rise again 45 minutes. Bake at 350 degrees 40 to 45 minutes. Let cool 5 minutes; then remove from oven.

makes 1 loaf

perfect dinner rolls

1 pkg active dry yeast
1/2 cup warm water
1 tbsp sugar
2 tbsps shortening
1 1/2 tsps salt
1/2 cup boiling water
3 1/2 to 3 3/4 cups all-purpose flour, sifted, divided
2 egg whites, stiffly beaten (reserve 1 yolk)
2 tbsps cornmeal
2 tsps water

issolve yeast in warm water. In large bowl combine sugar, shortening, salt, and boiling water. Cool until tepid, then add yeast mixture. Add 1 cup flour and egg whites, mixing thoroughly. Continue to add remaining cups flour to form stiff dough. Turn out dough and knead on floured surface until smooth, approximately 3 to 5 minutes. Place in greased bowl, cover, and put in warm place to rise, approximately 1 to 1 1/2 hours or until doubled. Shape into round rolls and dip bottoms in cornmeal. Place rolls on greased baking sheets and let rise in warm place another 1 to 1 1/2 hours. Brush tops of rolls with egg yolk mixed with water. Bake at 400 degrees 20 to 25 minutes.

makes 1 1/2 to 2 dozen

herb bread sticks

1 pkg active dry yeast
1 cup warm water
2 tbsps shortening, melted
1 tbsp sugar
1 1/2 tsps salt
2 tbsps chives, chopped
1 tbsp parsley, chopped
1 tsp dill seed
2 1/2 to 3 cups all-purpose flour, sifted
1 egg, slightly beaten
1/4 tsp caraway seed or to taste

In large bowl dissolve yeast in warm water. Mix in shortening, sugar, salt, chives, parsley, and dill seed. Gradually add flour to form stiff dough, mixing well after each addition. Cover and let rise in warm place for 1 hour or until doubled. Divide dough into four parts. Take one part and roll out on floured surface to 8-inch square. Cut into four 2-inch strips and twist each strip to form a stick. Place sticks on greased baking sheet and brush each with egg. Sprinkle each with salt and caraway seed. Repeat process until all dough is used. Set aside and let rise in warm place 30 to 45 minutes. Bake at 400 degrees 15 to 20 minutes.

makes 16

i must be dreamin' cheese buns

1 pkg active dry yeast
1/2 cup warm water
2/3 cup processed American cheese,
    shredded, or cheese spread
2 tbsps sugar
1 tsp salt
1 egg
2 tbsps butter, melted
2 1/4 to 2 1/2 cups all-purpose flour,
    sifted, divided

rease 12 muffin cups and set aside.
In large bowl dissolve yeast in warm water; let stand 5 minutes. Mix in shredded soft cheese or cheese spread, sugar, salt, egg, butter, and 1 cup flour. Beat until cheese is well blended. Add remaining flour gradually to form dough, mixing well after each addition. Fill muffin cups half full. Cover and put in warm place to rise, approximately 1 to 1 1/2 hours. Bake at 375 degrees 12 to 15 minutes.

1 dozen

2 pkgs active dry yeast
1 3/4 cups warm water
1/2 cup honey
1/4 cup shortening, melted
1 egg, well beaten
2 tsps salt
6 to 6 1/4 cups all-purpose flour, sifted, divided

honey rolls

makes 3 dozen

rease 3 dozen muffin cups and set aside. In large mixing bowl dissolve yeast in warm water. Mix in honey, shortening, egg, and salt, stirring well. Blend in 4 cups flour and beat about 1 minute. Add remaining cups flour to form stiff dough; beat well. (Dough can be refrigerated at this point up to 2 days.) Place in bowl and let rise in warm place approximately 1 to 1 1/2 hours or until doubled. Stir 1 minute and drop 2 spoonfuls into each muffin cup. Bake at 400 degrees 12 to 15 minutes.

dreamy cinnamon nut rolls

1 pkg active dry yeast
1/2 cup warm water
2 eggs, well beaten
1 cup cream, lukewarm
3 tbsps sugar, plus additional
   for sprinkling on rolls
1 1/2 tsps salt
1 tsp vanilla

4 1/2 to 5 cups all-purpose flour, sifted,
   plus additional for dipping
2 tbsps butter, melted
1 cup brown sugar, firmly packed
1 tsp cinnamon
2 tbsps butter, melted
3/4 cup nuts, finely chopped
1/3 cup raisins, chopped (optional)

makes about 2 dozen

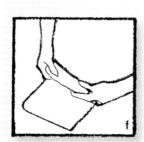

dissolve yeast in water. In large mixing bowl mix together eggs, cream, sugar, salt, and vanilla Gradually add flour to form stiff dough. Turn out on floured surface and knead approximately 2 to 3 minutes or until smooth. Place in greased bowl, cover, and put in warm place to rise, about 1 1/2 hours or until doubled. Turn out on floured surface and roll into 26 x 20-inch rectangle; brush with butter. Combine brown sugar and cinnamon; sprinkle half of mixture over dough. Fold in half lengthwise, pressing firmly. Fold in half again lengthwise and seal edges. Dough should be four layers deep.

Roll again into 26 x 12-inch rectangle; brush with butter. Combine nuts, raisins, and remaining brown sugar-cinnamon mixture and sprinkle over dough. Roll to resemble a jelly roll, starting with the longer side; slice into 1-inch slices. Dip one cut side of each roll in flour and place floured-side up on sugared surface. Roll to 1/4-inch thickness. Place on well-greased baking sheets, sugared-side up. Let rise in warm place at least 15 minutes. Bake at 375 degrees 15 to 18 minutes. (While first pans of rolls are baking, allow extra rolls to rise, sugared-side up.)

anytime bread twists

makes 2 dozen

2 pkgs active dry yeast
1/4 cup warm water
1/2 cup shortening
3 tbsps sugar
1 1/2 tsps salt
1 tsp vanilla
1/4 cup milk, heated to
    scalding

3 eggs
3 cups all-purpose
    flour, sifted, divided
3/4 cup nuts, chopped
1/2 cup sugar
1 tsp cinnamon

Soften yeast in warm water and set aside
In large mixing bowl combine shortening, sugar, salt, vanilla, and milk. Add yeast mixture and let stand 5 minutes. Gradually blend in 1 1/2 cups flour, mixing well until smooth. Cover and let stand 15 minutes. Add eggs one at a time, beating well after each. Add remaining 1 1/2 cups flour gradually; mix well to form soft dough. Cover and let rise in warm place about 30 minutes. In small mixing bowl combine nuts, sugar, and cinnamon. Using tablespoon divide dough into small pieces and roll each in sugar-nut mixture. Stretch each piece until it is about 8 inches long. Twist or tie into desired shape and place on greased baking sheet; let stand 5 minutes. Bake at 375 degrees 12 to 15 minutes.

easy nut knots

2 pkgs active dry yeast
1/4 cup warm water
1/3 cup butter
3/4 cup milk, heated to scalding
1/3 cup sugar
2 tsps salt
2 tsps orange rind, grated
2 eggs
4 to 4 1/2 cups all-purpose flour, sifted
filling (see left)
glaze (see left)

filling

1/3 cup butter
1 cup powdered sugar, sifted
1 cup nuts, finely chopped

To make filling:
Cream butter, blend in sugar, and stir in nuts.

glaze

1/4 cup orange juice
3 tbsps sugar

To make glaze:
Mix juice and sugar together.

Soften yeast in warm water and set aside. In large mixing bowl combine butter and milk; cool to lukewarm. Add sugar, salt, orange rind, eggs, and softened yeast. Gradually add flour, beating well to form stiff dough. Cover and let stand 30 minutes. On floured surface roll dough to approximately 22 x 12 inches. Spread filling over one-half of dough along 22-inch side. Fold other half on top of filling. Cut into 1-inch strips along the short (12-inch) side. Twist each strip a few times and "tie" one time to resemble a knot. Place each tied piece onto greased cookie sheet. Cover and let rise in warm place approximately 45 to 60 minutes or until doubled. Bake at 375 degrees 15 minutes. Brush glaze on top and bake another 5 minutes.

makes 1 1/2 to 2 dozen

best-ever egg bread

5 1/2 cups all-purpose flour, divided
2/3 cup sugar
1/2 tsp salt
2 pkgs dry active yeast
1/2 cup butter
1 cup milk
4 eggs
1 egg white, beaten

In large mixing bowl combine 2 cups flour, sugar, salt, and yeast. In saucepan melt butter, add milk, and warm thoroughly. Pour mixture over dry ingredients and mix well until smooth. Add eggs; gradually blend in enough flour to make soft dough. Place dough on floured surface and knead lightly. Turn into greased bowl, cover, and let rise in warm place until doubled in size, approximately one hour. Punch down. Place dough again on floured surface and knead gently. Shape into large round loaf and put on greased baking sheet. Cover and let rise an hour or until doubled. Brush dough with egg white. Place on bottom oven rack and bake at 325 degrees 50 to 55 minutes or until browned.

makes 1 loaf

carnival snack bread

1 pkg active dry yeast
1/4 cup warm water
1 tbsp sugar
2 tbsps shortening
1 1/4 tsps salt, divided
3/4 cup milk, heated to scalding
2 1/4 to **2 1/2** cups all-purpose flour
1 egg
1/3 cup milk
1 tsp onion, grated
2 cups American cheese, shredded
pinch of caraway seeds or dill seeds

Soften yeast in warm water; set aside. In large mixing bowl combine sugar, shortening, 1 teaspoon salt, and scalded milk; cool to lukewarm. Stir in yeast mixture. Add flour and blend well. Turn onto floured surface and knead until smooth, approximately 3 minutes. Put dough in greased bowl and cover. Let rise in warm place 1 to 1 1/2 hours or until doubled. Place dough in greased 15 x 10 x 1-inch pan. Let rise again in warm place 45 minutes. In small bowl combine egg, 1/3 cup milk, onion, remaining 1/4 teaspoon salt, and cheese. Spread mixture over dough and sprinkle with seeds. Bake at 425 degrees 15 to 20 minutes.

makes 1 large bread

herbed square bread

1 1/2 cups all-purpose flour
2 tbsps sugar
4 tsps baking powder
2 1/2 tsps salt
2 tsps sage
1 tsp thyme
1 1/2 cups cornmeal
1 1/2 cups onion, chopped
1 1/2 cups celery, chopped
3 eggs, beaten
1 1/2 cups milk
1/3 cup shortening, melted

In large mixing bowl sift together flour, sugar, baking powder, and salt. Stir in sage, thyme, cornmeal, onion, and celery; mix well. In small mixing bowl combine eggs, milk, and shortening; add to dry ingredients; stir only until blended. Pour into greased 9-inch square pan. Bake at 400 degrees 35 to 45 minutes.

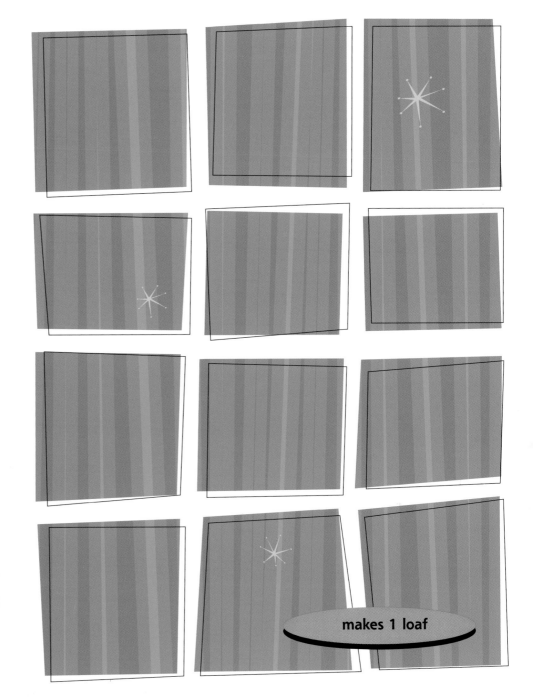

makes 1 loaf

sweet apple quick bread

2 cups all-purpose flour
1 cup sugar
1 tsp baking soda
1/2 tsp baking powder
1/2 tsp salt
1 cup (2 medium) apples, peeled
  and shredded
1/2 cup butter, softened
1/2 cup milk
2 tbsps orange peel, grated
1 tbsp corn syrup
2 eggs
1/2 cup nuts, chopped

in large bowl blend all ingredients except nuts. Beat 3 minutes at medium speed. Stir in nuts. Pour into greased loaf pan. Bake at 350 degrees 50 to 60 minutes.

makes 1 loaf

whole wheat brown bread

2 cups whole wheat flour
1/2 cup all-purpose flour
1 tsp baking powder
1 tsp baking soda
1 tsp salt
1 1/2 cups buttermilk
1/4 cup vegetable oil
1/4 cup honey
1/4 cup molasses

makes 1 loaf

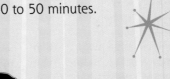

In large bowl combine all ingredients, beat until well moistened.
Pour into greased loaf pan. Bake at 350 degrees 40 to 50 minutes.

topping-of-the-morning breakfast bread

makes 1 loaf

2 cups all-purpose flour
2 1/2 tsps baking powder
1 tsp salt
1 cup sugar
1 egg, lightly beaten
3/4 cup milk
1 tbsp orange rind, grated
1/4 cup orange juice
1 tsp vanilla
1/4 cup butter, melted
1/4 cup shortening, melted
topping (see below)

n large mixing bowl sift together flour, baking powder, salt, and sugar. Make a well in center and add rest of ingredients, mixing well until blended. Grease only the bottom of 13 x 9-inch pan and pour in batter evenly; spoon topping evenly over batter. Bake at 400 degrees 30 to 40 minutes.

topping

2 1/2 cups (3 medium) apples, peeled and grated
1 tbsp orange juice
1/4 cup brown sugar, firmly packed
1 tsp cinnamon
10 maraschino cherries, drained, and chopped
2 tbsps butter, melted

To make topping:
In small mixing bowl combine all ingredients and mix well.

savory bakery

Baking, of course, is not limited to breads or sweets. The savory side of baking is just as important to cooks and families as filling the bread board or the cookie jar. The creation of hearty, wholesome main meals is the mainstay of family life.

Not many generations ago, life was work-centered and leisure time was minimal. The majority of hours in a day were spent farming, working in the factory, or managing domestic chores; it was a welcome respite when the mealtime bell rang. Supper or dinner was the focal point of the day—a time to rest for a few moments and unwind. For many rural families, the noon meal served as the big meal of the day. Work stopped and a homemade, fortifying meal was provided for those laboring in the fields. Urban families waited until Father came home in the early evening; then the entire household enjoyed a hearty meal together.

These designated mealtimes fed the body as well as the soul and were of great social importance. Coming together to eat provided the opportunity to share news of the day and build family relationships. Recipes like piping bacon corn bake or spicy chili cheese bake created a sense of home as much as they enticed family members to the table.

Although my workdays are not spent in a field or factory, I have spent countless hours judging a variety of recipe contests. As I peruse through hundreds and sometimes thousands of entries, I am often challenged to find those few special recipes that are considered the best. I often search for recipes that have interesting uses of ingredients or unique preparation methods. Most of all, however, I look for recipes that combine these things with broad family appeal – delicious, tasty dishes that offer today's taste with the simplicity of yesterday.

Gather the family and reconnect with a slower, more relaxed time. With the help of the satisfying meals showcased in this chapter, you will not regret it!

hearty veggie-beef bake

1 cup all-purpose flour, sifted
1 tsp salt
3 eggs, beaten
1 cup milk
1 tbsp butter, melted
12 to 18 2-inch square
   of cheese
filling (see right)

serves 6 to 8

Sift together flour and salt. In large mixing bowl combine eggs, milk, and butter. Gradually add dry ingredients; beat well. Fill well-greased muffin cups two-thirds full. Bake at 425 degrees 15 minutes. Reduce oven temperature to 325 degrees and bake an additional 30 to 35 minutes. Prick each muffin with sharp knife and top with 2-inch square of cheese. Bake another 2 to 5 minutes or until cheese melts. Remove from pans and cut in half. Spoon filling over top and serve.

To make filling:
In skillet brown beef; add green pepper and onion; cook until onion is transparent. Mix in flour until all pieces are coated. Add soup, celery, carrots, chili powder, and salt, mixing until well blended. Cover and simmer 20 minutes.

filling

1 pound ground beef
2 tbsps green pepper, chopped
2 tbsps onion, chopped
2 tbsps all-purpose flour
1 10 1/2-oz. can condensed tomato soup
1/2 cup celery, finely diced
1/2 cup carrots, finely diced
1/2 tsp chili powder
1 tsp salt

chili cheese bake

in skillet melt 1/4 cup shortening. Add onion, beef, 3 tablespoons flour, 1 teaspoon salt, and 1 teaspoon chili powder; brown well. Put in ungreased 2-quart casserole. In saucepan melt remaining 1/4 cup shortening and combine with remaining 1/3 cup flour, remaining 1 teaspoon salt, remaining teaspoon chili powder, and paprika. Slowly blend in milk; cook and stir constantly until thick. Stir in cheese until melted and remove from heat. Slowly blend small portion of hot mixture into egg yolks. Add back into hot mixture, blending well. In small mixing bowl beat egg whites until stiff peaks form. Fold into cheese mixture and pour over mixture in casserole. Place casserole in pan of hot water and bake at 350 degrees 50 to 60 minutes. Serve immediately.

serves 4 to 6

- 1/2 cup shortening, divided
- 1/4 cup onion, chopped
- 1 pound lean ground beef
- 3 tbsps plus 1/3 cup all-purpose flour, divided
- 2 tsps salt, divided
- 2 tsps chili powder, divided
- 1/8 tsp paprika
- 1 1/2 cups milk
- 2 cups American cheese, shredded
- 4 egg yolks, slightly beaten
- 4 egg whites

parmesan cheese chops

4 pork chops (center cut works best)
1/2 cup all-purpose flour
1/2 tsp baking powder
2 tbsps shortening
2/3 cup milk
2 eggs
1/3 cup Parmesan cheese, grated
2 tbsps onion, grated
1/2 tsp salt
1/4 tsp pepper
pinch of paprika

n heavy 10-inch skillet quickly brown pork chops on one side; drain off fat. Turn chops over so browned sides are up. Sift together flour and baking powder. In saucepan melt shortening and blend in flour mixture. Gradually add milk, mixing well. Cook over medium heat, stirring constantly, until thick. Remove from heat and blend in eggs. Continue cooking over low heat, beating mixture until very thick. Remove from heat and add cheese, onion, salt, and pepper; mix well. Cover chops with cheese mixture and top with paprika. Bake at 350 degrees about 1 hour.

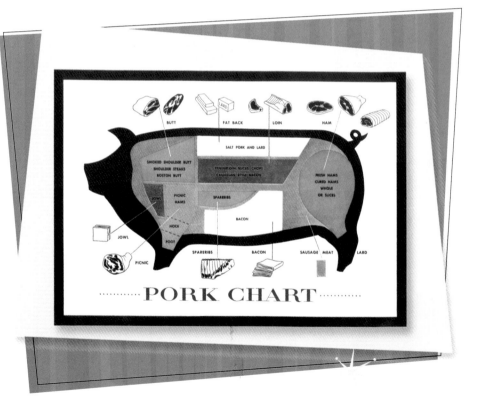

PORK CHART

aunt patty's meal-in-one pork bake

2 cups (1 pound) pork, cubed
1 tbsp shortening
1/4 cup green pepper, chopped
1/2 cup water
2 cups (two 8-oz. cans) tomato sauce
2 cups whole-kernel corn (frozen or canned)
1/2 cup all-purpose flour
1 tbsp sugar
2 tsps baking powder
3/4 tsp salt
1/2 cup yellow cornmeal
1 egg, well beaten
1/2 cup milk
2 tbsps shortening, melted

serves 6 to 8

In skillet brown pork cubes in shortening; cook until tender. In small saucepan simmer green pepper in water until tender; drain and set aside. In 2-quart casserole combine tomato sauce, corn, and cooked pork. In large mixing bowl sift together flour, sugar, baking powder, and salt. Add cornmeal and stir until blended. In small mixing bowl beat together egg, milk, and shortening; stir in cooked green pepper. Add to dry ingredients, mixing just until smooth. Pour over hot pork mixture and bake at 400 degrees 25 to 30 minutes.

veal and dumpling casserole

1/3 cup all-purpose flour
1 tsp paprika
2 pounds veal round steak, cut into 2-inch pieces
1/4 cup vegetable oil
1/2 tsp salt
1/8 tsp pepper
2 3/4 cups water, divided
1 10 1/2-oz. can condensed cream of chicken soup
1 3/4 cups small onions, cooked
dumplings (see below)
sauce (see below)

serves 6 to 8

n shallow dish mix together flour and paprika; dredge veal strips to cover evenly. In medium skillet brown veal in oil. Add salt, pepper, and 1 cup water. Cover and simmer 30 minutes or until tender. Transfer to 3-quart casserole or two smaller casseroles. In same skillet veal was browned in, heat soup. Gradually blend in remaining 1 3/4 cups water; bring to boil, stirring constantly. Combine with meat mixture. Add onions and top with dumplings. Bake uncovered at 425 degrees for 20 to 25 minutes. Serve with sauce.

sauce

1 10 1/2-oz. can condensed cream of chicken soup
1 cup sour cream

To make sauce:
In saucepan combine soup and sour cream and heat to boiling.

dumplings

2 cups all-purpose flour
4 tsps baking powder
1/2 tsp salt
1 tsp poultry seasoning
1 tsp celery seed
1 tsp dry onion flakes
1 tsp poppy seed, if desired
1/4 cup salad oil
1 cup milk
1/4 cup butter, melted
1 cup bread crumbs

To make dumplings:
In large mixing bowl sift together flour, baking powder, salt, and poultry seasoning. Stir in celery seed, onion flakes, and poppy seed, if desired. Add oil and milk, mixing until just moistened. In small bowl mix together melted butter and bread crumbs. Roll tablespoons of dough in crumb mixture to coat well.

chicken cheese pie

1 cup all-purpose flour
1/2 tsp salt
1/3 cup shortening
1 egg, divided
2 tbsps water
filling (see right)

serves 6

In mixing bowl mix together flour and salt. With pastry cutter or fork, cut in shortening until mixture becomes crumbly. In small bowl beat egg slightly. Mix 1 tablespoon of beaten egg with water, reserving remainder of egg for filling. Sprinkle egg and water mixture over sifted flour; stir with fork until dough holds together. Form into ball and roll on floured surface to a circle about 1 inch larger than top of 9-inch pie pan. Place dough in pie pan, fold edges over, and flute to make rim. With fork prick dough generously. Bake at 425 degrees 8 minutes.

filling

1/2 cup onion, chopped
2 tbsps green pepper, chopped
1/4 cup butter
2 tbsps all-purpose flour
1/2 cup chicken broth
3 cups chicken, cooked and cubed
3/4 cup carrots, cooked and diced
8 slices (1/2 pound) American cheese

To make filling:

In medium skillet sauté onion and green pepper in butter until tender. Stir in flour and chicken broth; cook until thickened. Add chicken, carrots, and reserved egg. Pour into pie shell and top with cheese. Bake at 400 degrees 20 to 25 minutes.

chicken crepes

1 cup whipping cream
6 eggs
1 tbsp sugar
1/2 tsp salt
2 tsps grated orange rind
1 cup all-purpose flour, sifted
3 tbsps butter, melted
filling (see below)
sauce (see below)

In medium mixing bowl beat cream until thick. In small mixing bowl combine eggs, sugar, salt, and orange rind; beat well. Fold mixture into whipped cream. Gradually add flour, mixing well after each addition; stir in butter. Pour 1/4 cup batter in hot skillet, spread into 6-inch pancake, and cook until light brown on each side. Spread heaping tablespoon of filling into each crepe. Roll up and place in greased rectangle baking dish; spoon sauce over top, and bake at 450 degrees 10 minutes.

filling

1/2 cup mushrooms, chopped
5 tbsps butter
1/3 cup all-purpose flour, sifted
2 cups milk
3 cups chicken, cooked and finely chopped
1 tsp salt
1/8 tsp pepper

To make filling:
In medium skillet sauté mushrooms in butter until tender. Blend in flour and gradually add milk. Cook until thickened, stirring constantly. Add chicken, salt, and pepper; mix well.

sauce

1 cup butter
6 egg yolks
1 tsp salt
1/8 tsp pepper
3 tbsps lemon juice
1 cup boiling water

serves 6 to 8

To make sauce:
In small saucepan cream butter. Add egg yolks one at a time; beat well after each one. Mix in salt, pepper, and lemon juice. Slowly add boiling water and beat well. Cook over low heat, stirring constantly, 5 minutes.

36

coastal crab pie

1 cup all-purpose flour
1/2 tsp salt
1/3 cup shortening
3 to 4 tbsps cold water
filling (see below)
sauce (see below)

serves 6

I n medium mixing bowl sift together flour and salt. With pastry cutter or fork, cut in shortening until mixture becomes crumbly. Sprinkle water over mixture while stirring lightly with a fork. Keep mixing until dough sticks together. Form dough into ball and roll on floured surface to a circle about 1 inch larger than top rim of pie pan. Place dough in pie pan. Fold over edge and flute to form upright rim. Prick dough generously with fork. Bake at 450 degrees 10 to 12 minutes. Fill with crab filling and top with sauce. Reduce oven temperature to 400 degrees and bake 25 to 30 minutes.

filling

2 cups (two 6 1/2-oz. cans) crabmeat
2/3 cup chili sauce
1/4 to 1/2 cup green pepper, chopped
1/2 cup celery, chopped
1/4 tsp salt
1 1/2 tsps onion, grated

To make filling:
In medium mixing bowl combine all ingredients and stir until well blended.

sauce

3 tbsps butter
3 tbsps all-purpose flour
1/4 tsp salt
1/2 tsp Worcestershire sauce
1/2 cup milk
1 cup American cheese, shredded

To make sauce:
In small saucepan melt butter over medium heat. Blend in flour, salt, Worcestershire sauce, and milk. Cook, stirring constantly, until thickened. Stir in cheese until melted.

northwest's best salmon pie

1 cup all-purpose flour, sifted
1/2 tsp salt
1/3 cup shortening
3 to 4 tbsps cold water
filling (see below)
sauce (see below)

serves 4 to 6

In medium mixing bowl sift together flour and salt. With pastry cutter or fork, cut in shortening until mixture becomes crumbly. Sprinkle water over mixture while stirring lightly with fork. Keep mixing until dough sticks together. Form dough into ball and roll on floured surface to a circle about 1 inch larger than top rim of pie pan. Place dough in pie pan. Fold over edge and flute to form upright rim. Bake at 450 degrees 10 to 12 minutes. Pour in filling, reduce oven temperature to 425 degrees, and bake 20 to 25 minutes. Serve hot with sauce.

First you Catch your Fish

filling

1 can (1 pound) salmon, cooked
3 eggs, beaten
1/4 cup butter, melted
2 tsps minced parsley (fresh or dried)
1/4 tsp salt
1/4 tsp basil, if desired

To make filling:
In medium mixing bowl flake salmon (be sure to remove skin and bones). Add eggs, butter, parsley, salt, and basil, if desired; stir well.

sauce

1/3 cup cucumber, grated
1 tsp onion, minced
1/4 cup mayonnaise
2 tsps vinegar
1/2 cup sour cream
2 tsps parsley, minced
1/16 tsp each salt and pepper

To make sauce:
Press cucumber and onion in wire strainer to remove juice. In small mixing bowl place drained cucumber and onion; add mayonnaise, vinegar, sour cream, parsley, salt, and pepper; mix well.

bacon corn bake

1/2 **pound bacon**
2 **cups all-purpose flour**
1/4 **tsp salt**
6 to 7 **tsps cold milk**
pinch of paprika, if desired
filling (see right)

in medium skillet fry bacon until crisp. Remove bacon and drain on paper towels; reserve drippings. Crumble bacon and set aside. In large mixing bowl sift together flour and salt. Mix in 1/2 cup bacon drippings, stirring only until all dry particles are moistened. Sprinkle milk over mixture, stirring with fork until dough sticks together. Divide dough in half and form each into ball. On floured surface roll one half into circle about 1 inch larger than top rim of pie pan. Place dough evenly in pie pan. Pour filling into pie shell. Roll remaining dough into circle large enough to cover pie. Dampen rim of bottom crust and place top crust over filling. Fold edge of top crust under edge of bottom crust; seal edge and flute. Cut slits in top crust to vent steam. Bake at 400 degrees 45 to 60 minutes. Top with paprika, if desired.

filling

1 **10-oz. pkg frozen whole-kernel corn, thawed**
  (or 2 cups canned corn)
1/4 **cup green pepper, chopped**
1/4 **cup onion, chopped**
3 **hard-cooked eggs, chopped**
1 **10 1/2-oz. can condensed cream of celery soup**
1/2 **tsp salt**

To make filling:
Combine corn, green pepper, onion, eggs, soup, salt, and reserved crumbled bacon.

serves 4 to 6

quick-n-easy casserole

1/2 cup all-purpose flour
2 tsps salt
1 tsp baking powder
2 tsps chili powder
1/4 tsp pepper
1 cup cornmeal
3 1/2 cups (two 16-oz. cans) cream-
  style corn
1 cup (8-oz. can) tomato sauce
1 cup milk
1/2 cup shortening, melted
2 eggs, beaten
1 cup black olives, sliced or chopped
2 tbsps onion, minced

serves 4 to 6

I'M FLABBERGASTED

In large mixing bowl sift together flour, salt, baking powder, chili powder, and pepper; stir in cornmeal. In medium mixing bowl combine corn, tomato sauce, milk, shortening, and eggs. Add to dry ingredients; mix well until thoroughly blended. Add olives and onion; stir well. Pour into greased 2-quart casserole and bake at 350 degrees 60 to 90 minutes.

bacon spinach pie

one-crust pastry

1 cup flour
1/2 tsp salt
1/3 cup butter or shortening
glass of ice water

To make pastry:

Mix flour and salt in medium mixing bowl. Use pastry cutter to blend in butter or shortening until mixture becomes crumbly. Add 3 to 4 table-spoons of ice water one at a time until dough is moist enough to form into a ball. Flatten ball to 1/2-inch thickness, smooth rough edges, and roll out onto floured surface. Dough should form even circle 1 1/2 inches larger than a 8- or 9-inch pie pan. Place crust loosely in pan, pat out air pockets, fold and flute edge to form even rim. Prick crust generously with fork and bake at 450 degrees for 10 to 12 minutes. Allow to cool before filling.

one-crust pastry (see right)
6 strips bacon
3 cups fresh spinach, chopped (or one 12-oz. pkg frozen chopped spinach, thawed and thoroughly drained)
3 eggs
2 tsps sugar
1 tsp salt
1/4 tsp onion salt
1/8 tsp pepper
pinch cayenne pepper, if desired
2 cups hot milk
1 cup (1/4 pound) American or cheddar cheese, shredded

serves 6

Prepare recipe for one-crust pastry, using 9-inch pie pan. In medium skillet fry bacon until crisp; add spinach and set aside. In large mixing bowl combine eggs, sugar, salt, onion salt, pepper, and cayenne pepper, if desired; stir in milk. Evenly spread spinach and bacon on bottom of pie shell. Pour egg mixture over spinach and top with cheese. Bake at 400 degrees 25 to 30 minutes.

carmelized onion pie

1 1/2 pounds (5 to 6 medium) onions, diced
3 tbsp olive oil
2 tbsp butter
1/2 cup roasted red bell pepper, finely chopped
2 eggs
1 cup sour cream
1 tsp salt
1/8 tsp pepper
crust (see right)
topping (see below)

crust

1 1/2 cups all-purpose flour
1/2 tsp salt
1 tsp onion powder
1/2 cup shortening
1/4 cup cold water
1 egg white, slightly beaten

In medium mixing bowl blend together flour, salt, and onion powder. Using pastry cutter or fork, cut in shortening until flour mixture becomes crumbly. Sprinkle cold water over flour mixture, stirring with fork until moistened. On floured surface roll out and line 9-inch pie pan. Flute edges and brush entire shell with egg white.

In medium skillet cook onions in oil over medium heat until caramel in color, approximately 30 to 35 minutes; stir frequently. When onions are caramelized, add butter and bell pepper; stir until butter is melted; remove from heat. In large bowl mix together eggs, sour cream, salt, and pepper. Add onion mixture and mix thoroughly. Pour into pie shell. Place on bottom oven rack and bake at 350 degrees 40 to 45 minutes. Sprinkle topping on cooked pie and serve.

topping

1 tsp butter
1/2 cup pine nuts
1 tbsp chives, finely chopped

To make topping:

In small skillet melt butter. Add pine nuts and sauté over medium heat until lightly browned. Drain on paper towel and cool. Finely chop nuts and mix with chives.

serves 6 to 8

hungry-man beef casserole

1 pound round steak,
   cut into 1/2-inch strips
1/4 cup shortening
1 1/2 cups onion, chopped
2 tbsps all-purpose flour
1 cup canned tomatoes
1 cup water
1 6-oz. can tomato paste
1 tbsp sugar
1 1/2 tsps salt
1/4 tsp pepper
1/2 tsp Worcestershire sauce
1 cup mushrooms, sliced
3/4 cup sour cream
biscuits (see below)

In large skillet brown steak in shortening. Add onion and flour; mix well. Continue cooking until onions are tender, stirring often. Stir in tomatoes, water, tomato paste, sugar, salt, pepper, and Worcestershire sauce. Turn heat down, cover, and simmer until meat is tender, approximately 1 hour. Mix in mushrooms and sour cream; cook another 5 minutes. Place mixture in 2-quart casserole. Top with biscuits and bake uncovered at 425 degrees 20 to 25 minutes or until biscuits are golden brown.

biscuits

1 1/4 cups all-purpose flour
2 tsps baking powder
1/2 tsp salt
1/4 cup shortening
3/4 cup sour cream

Sift together flour, baking powder, and salt. With fork cut in shortening until mixture becomes crumbly. Mix in sour cream until dough becomes a ball. On floured surface roll dough to 3/4-inch thick and cut into 8 round biscuits.

serves 6 to 8

south-of-the-border beef pie

1 cup all-purpose flour
2 tbsps cornmeal
1/3 cup shortening
3 to 4 tbsps water
filling (see below)
topping (see right)
tomato sauce or salsa (optional)

serves 6

topping

1 egg
1/4 cup milk
1/2 tsp salt
1/2 tsp Worcestershire sauce
1 1/2 cups cheddar cheese, shredded

To make topping:
In small mixing bowl mix together all ingredients.

In small mixing bowl combine flour and cornmeal. Using fork cut in shortening until mixure becomes crumbly. Sprinkle water over mixture, stirring with fork until dough sticks together. On floured surface roll to circle approximately 1 inch larger than top rim of 9-inch pie pan. Place dough in pan; fold edge over, and flute to make standing rim. Place filling in pastry-lined pan. Bake at 425 degrees 25 minutes. Spread topping on pie and top with reserved bacon pieces. Bake another 5 minutes or until cheese melts. Let stand 10 minutes before serving. Serve with tomato sauce or salsa, if desired.

filling

6 slices bacon
1 pound ground beef
1 8-oz. can corn, drained
1/4 cup bell pepper, finely chopped
1/4 cup onion, finely chopped
1/4 cup cornmeal
1/2 tsp oregano
1/2 tsp chili powder
1/2 tsp salt
1/8 tsp pepper
1 8-oz. can tomato sauce

To make filling:
Fry bacon until crisp; remove, break into large pieces, and set aside. Brown beef in remaining bacon fat and drain. Stir in corn, bell pepper, onion, cornmeal, oregano, chili powder, salt, pepper, and tomato sauce.

cookies

Cookies are a personal favorite; my cookie jar just can't be empty. I'm sure this harks back to my childhood, when warm, freshly baked cookies were plentiful after school. Running home was worth the sideache it caused!

With mom staying at home in the 1940s and 1950s, keeping the cookie jar filled with all types of delicious treats was expected. Mrs. Ruth Wakefield, inventor of the famous Toll House Cookies, could not have known what she started when she dropped some chopped chocolate into a bowl of butter cookie dough. Her kitchen experiment created a whole new American mainstay and a favorite childhood memory.

Cookies have always expressed the fanciful and whimsical side of baking. With lighthearted names like blossoms, thins, crisps, twirls, and crinkles, cookies fulfill a creative outlet. Early cookie bakers brought their recipes from other countries and adapted them to ingredients found in the United States. These "little cakes," from the Dutch word koekje, were small and sweet so they could be made in a limited amount of time with few ingredients. As people moved westward with the railroad, bakers had more ingredients to choose from. Cookies took a different twist in the 1930s with the introduction of electric refrigerators for American kitchens. Icebox cookies, using cookie dough that is refrigerated and then sliced before baking, were especially popular.

There are as many different types of cookies as there are occasions: drop cookies, bars, cutouts, shaped, decorated, and refrigerated, to name a few. Whether everyday or extraordinary, cookies were highlighted at Victorian ice cream socials, packed for picnics, shared as schoolhouse treats, sold at bake sales and summer lemonade stands, mailed to homesick GIs, served at birthday parties, and, of course, savored after school, fresh from the oven.

Stir your memories (with a glass of cold milk) as you look through this chapter for your personal cookie favorites. These petite sweets are simply the best, and you may be pleasantly surprised to find that your favorite is a beloved cookie from days gone by.

frosted fudge wafers

3/4 cup all-purpose flour
1 tsp baking powder
1/4 tsp salt
1/2 cup butter
2 squares (2 oz.) unsweetened
  chocolate
1 cup sugar
2 eggs
1/2 tsp vanilla
1 cup nuts, chopped and divided
frosting (see below)

In small mixing bowl sift together flour, baking powder, and salt. In saucepan melt butter and chocolate over low heat; stir constantly. Remove from heat and beat in sugar, eggs, and vanilla. Blend in dry ingredients and 1/2 cup nuts; mix thoroughly. Spread into greased 15 1/2 x 10 1/2 x 1-inch baking pan. Bake at 375 degrees 17 to 20 minutes. Cool and frost; sprinkle with remaining 1/2 cup nuts. When frosting is set, cut into squares.

COOKY JAR FILLED

frosting

1 tbsp butter
1 square unsweetened chocolate
1/4 cup water
1 1/2 cups powdered sugar, sifted
1/2 tsp almond extract

To make frosting:
In small saucepan over low heat, melt butter and chocolate in water. Remove from heat; add powdered sugar and almond extract.

makes about 3 dozen

chocolate peanut bars

makes about 2 1/2 dozen

2 cups all-purpose flour
1 tsp baking soda
1/2 tsp salt
1/2 cup butter
1/2 cup sugar
1 1/2 cups brown sugar, firmly packed and divided
1 cup (6-oz. pkg) semisweet chocolate pieces
3/4 cup salted peanuts, chopped and divided
2 eggs, separated
1 tsp vanilla

n small mixing bowl sift together flour, baking soda, and salt. In medium mixing bowl cream butter; gradually add sugar and 1/2 cup brown sugar; beat well. Stir in flour mixture. Press dough into greased 13 x 9 x 2-inch pan. Sprinkle chocolate and 1/2 cup peanuts over dough and pat in gently. In small mixing bowl beat egg whites until slight mounds form. Gradually mix in remaining 1 cup brown sugar; beat until stiff, straight peaks form. Spread over chocolate pieces. Sprinkle with remaining 1/4 cup peanuts; press into meringue slightly. Bake at 325 degrees 40 to 45 minutes. While warm, cut into bars.

sweet oat brownies

1/3 cup all-purpose flour

1/4 tsp baking soda

1/8 tsp salt

1/2 cup brown sugar, firmly packed

1 cup quick-cooking rolled oats

1/3 cup butter, melted

brownies (see right)

makes 1 1/2 dozen

In medium mixing bowl sift together flour, baking soda, and salt. Stir in sugar and oats; mix well. Blend in butter until mixture is crumbly. Press into ungreased 8 x 8 x 2-inch square pan. Bake at 350 degrees 10 minutes. Create brownie layer and follow baking instructions.

brownies

2/3 cup all-purpose flour

1/4 tsp baking soda

1/4 tsp salt

1 square (1 oz.) unsweetened chocolate

1/4 cup butter

3/4 cup sugar

1 egg

2 tbsps milk

1 tsp vanilla

To make brownies:

In small mixing bowl sift together flour, baking soda, and salt. In double boiler melt together chocolate and butter over hot water. Remove from heat and gradually blend in sugar. Beat in egg, mixing well. Stir in dry ingredients; mix thoroughly. Blend in milk and vanilla. Spread over crust and bake at 350 degrees 30 to 35 minutes.

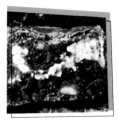

chocolate dough

1 cup all-purpose flour

1 tsp salt

3/4 cup sugar

1/2 cup shortening

1 egg

2 squares (2 oz.) unsweetened
chocolate, melted

1 tsp vanilla

peanut butter dough (see below)

choco-peanut sandwich cookies

makes about 3 1/2 dozen

In small mixing bowl sift together flour and salt; set aside. In medium bowl gradually add sugar to shortening; beat well. Blend in egg, chocolate, and vanilla; mix well. Add dry ingredients and mix thoroughly. Create peanut butter dough. On ungreased baking sheets drop half of chocolate dough by teaspoonfuls. Top each with the same amount of peanut butter dough, then with the same amount of chocolate dough, forming a sandwich. Press down with palm of hand. Bake at 325 degrees 12 to 15 minutes.

peanut butter dough

2 tbsps butter

1/4 cup peanut butter

1/2 cup brown sugar, firmly packed

2 tbsps all-purpose flour

To make peanut butter dough:

In small mixing bowl cream together butter and peanut butter. Gradually add brown sugar and beat well. Blend in flour and mix thoroughly.

lemon wafers

1/2 cup butter
3/4 cup brown sugar, firmly packed
1 egg
3/4 cup all-purpose flour, sifted
1/2 cup almonds, finely chopped
1/4 cup quick-cooking rolled oats
1 tbsp lemon rind, grated
1/2 tsp lemon extract

In small mixing bowl cream butter; gradually add brown sugar and cream well. Beat in egg; stir in flour. Mix in almonds, oats, lemon rind, and lemon extract. Drop by teaspoonfuls 3 inches apart onto greased baking sheets. Bake at 350 degrees 7 to 10 minutes.

makes 3 dozen

crunchy cashew cookies

2 1/4 cups all-purpose flour
1/2 tsp baking soda
1/2 tsp cream of tartar
1 cup butter
3/4 cup brown sugar, firmly packed
1/2 cup sugar
1 egg
1 tsp vanilla
1 1/2 cups (7 oz.) cashew or peanut crunch candy, finely crushed

in small mixing bowl sift together flour, baking soda, and cream of tartar. In medium mixing bowl cream butter. Gradually add sugars; beat well. Mix in egg and vanilla; gradually add dry ingredients and mix thoroughly. Fold in nut crunch candy. Drop by rounded teaspoonfuls onto greased baking sheets. Bake at 350 degrees 12 to 15 minutes.

makes about 5 dozen

peanut blossoms

makes about 3 dozen

1 3/4 cups all-purpose flour
1 tsp baking soda
1/2 tsp salt
1/2 cup shortening
1/2 cup peanut butter
1/2 cup sugar
1/2 cup brown sugar, firmly packed
1 egg
1 tsp vanilla
sugar for rolling
1 pkg (at least 36 pieces) solid milk chocolate candy kisses

In small mixing bowl sift together flour, baking soda, and salt. In medium mixing bowl cream together shortening and peanut butter. Gradually add sugars; beat well. Add egg and vanilla; beat well. Add dry ingredients and mix thoroughly. Using teaspoon, shape dough into balls and roll in sugar. Place on greased baking sheets and bake at 375 degrees 10 minutes. Remove from oven and top each with candy kiss; press down firmly until cookie cracks around edge. Return to oven and bake another 2 to 5 minutes.

pecan topper cookies

1 1/2 cups all-purpose flour

1/4 tsp baking soda

1/4 tsp salt

1/2 cup butter

1/2 cup brown sugar, firmly packed

1 egg

1 egg, separated

1/4 tsp vanilla

1 bag pecan halves

frosting (see below)

In small mixing bowl sift together flour, baking soda, and salt. In medium mixing bowl cream butter. Gradually add sugar and cream well. Mix in egg, egg yolk, and vanilla; beat well. Mix in dry ingredients; stir well. Shape by rounded teaspoonfuls into balls; dip bottoms into unbeaten egg white and press lightly onto greased cookie sheet. Bake at 350 degrees 10 to 13 minutes. Cool and frost tops with frosting; press pecan half in top center of cookie.

frosting

2 squares (2 oz.) unsweetened
chocolate (or 1/3 cup semisweet
chocolate pieces)

1/4 cup milk

1 tbsp butter

1 cup powdered sugar

To make frosting:
In double boiler melt chocolate in milk and butter; blend until smooth. Remove from heat and add sugar; beat until smooth and glossy.

makes 2 1/2 dozen

super sugar cookies

2 cups all-purpose flour
2/3 cup sugar
1 tsp salt
1/2 cup shortening
1/4 cup butter
1 tbsp milk
3 tbsps boiling water
2 egg yolks
2 tsps lemon rind, grated
1 tsp vanilla
glaze (see below)

makes 4 dozen

In small mixing bowl sift together flour, sugar, and salt. In medium mixing bowl blend shortening, butter, milk, and boiling water. Beat in egg yolks, lemon rind, and vanilla; mix thoroughly. Gradually add dry ingredients and stir to form dough. Chill about 1 hour. On floured surface roll half the dough to about 1/8-inch thick. Cut into desired shapes and place on ungreased baking sheets. Bake at 400 degrees 6 to 9 minutes. Cool and frost with glaze.

glaze

1 cup powdered sugar, sifted
2 tbsps cream
1/2 tsp vanilla

To make glaze:
In small mixing bowl blend all ingredients; beat until smooth.

spiced cookies

2 cups brown sugar; firmly packed
1/2 cup butter, softened
1/2 cup shortening
2 eggs
1 tsp vanilla
3 cups all-purpose flour
1 tsp baking soda
1 tsp cream of tartar
1/2 tsp salt
1 cup quick oats
1/2 cup pecans, chopped
1/2 cup sugar
4 tsps cinnamon

makes 8 to 9 dozen

In large mixing bowl blend brown sugar, butter, shortening, eggs, and vanilla; beat well. Add flour, baking soda, cream of tartar, and salt; mix thoroughly. Fold in oats and pecans. Divide dough into thirds, shaping each section into a log about 12 inches long. Wrap in waxed paper and chill dough 6 hours or overnight. In small bowl mix together sugar and cinnamon. Slice cookies 1/4-inch thick and dip each flat side in sugar-cinnamon mixture. Place on greased cookie sheets and bake at 350 degrees 9 to 12 minutes.

brown sugar cookies

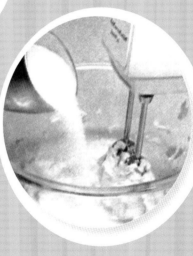

1 cup butter
3/4 cup sugar, divided
1/2 cup dark brown sugar
1 egg
1 tsp vanilla
2 cups all-purpose flour
1/2 cup pecans, chopped
1 tsp salt
1/2 tsp baking soda

In medium mixing bowl cream together butter, 1/2 cup sugar, and brown sugar. Beat in egg and vanilla. In small mixing bowl combine flour, pecans, salt, and baking soda; add into creamed mixture and mix well. Cover and refrigerate 20 minutes or until dough becomes easy to handle. Using teaspoon shape dough into 1-inch balls and roll in remaining 1/4 cup sugar. Place on ungreased baking sheet 2 inches apart. Flatten with bottom of flat-bottomed glass dipped in sugar. Bake at 350 degrees 10 to 12 minutes or until edges are slightly browned.

makes about 5 dozen

cheese ringers

1/2 pound (2 cups) cheddar or
   American cheese, shredded
1 cup butter, softened
3 1/2 cups flour, sifted
frosting (see below)

Preheat oven to 425 degrees. In a mixing bowl blend together cheese and butter. Gradually add flour and mix to form a stiff dough. Separate dough into two halves and roll each into a log about 12 inches long. Wrap and refrigerate for a few hours. Slice dough to approximately 1/4-inch thick and place on baking sheets. Bake for 8 to 12 minutes. Cool on wire rack and frost, if desired.

frosting

3 tsps butter, softened
3 tsps orange juice
1 1/2 tsps lemon juice
1 1/2 cups powdered sugar, sifted
1 tbsp cream

To make frosting:
In a small bowl mix together butter, orange juice, and lemon juice. Beat in powdered sugar and cream. If necessary, thin with milk or additional cream.

makes 8 to 10 dozen

wishbone cookies

1 pkg active dry yeast
1/4 cup warm water
2 1/2 cups all-purpose flour
1 cup sugar, divided
1 1/2 tsps salt
1/2 cup butter
1/4 cup shortening
2 eggs, separated (reserve whites)
1/4 cup cream
1 tsp almond extract
1 1/4 cups pecans, finely chopped, divided
2 tsps instant coffee
1 tbsp water

issolve yeast in warm water and set aside. In small mixing bowl sift together flour, 1/4 cup sugar, and salt. In medium mixing bowl cream together butter and shortening. Mix in egg yolks, cream, and almond extract; beat well. Add yeast mixture, flour mixture, and 1/2 cup pecans; mix well. Chill at least 1 hour. In small mixing bowl combine remaining 3/4 cup sugar, 3/4 cup pecans, and coffee. Using teaspoon form dough into balls and roll into 6-inch strips approximately 1/2 inch in diameter. In small bowl lightly beat egg whites and water. Dip dough sticks into egg whites and coat with sugar mixture. Form a "V" with the dough and place on greased baking sheet. Press bottom of the "V" together so it looks like a wishbone. Bake at 400 degrees 12 to 14 minutes.

makes about 3 dozen

chocolate chip oatmeal cookies

1 cup butter, softened
1 cup brown sugar, packed
1/2 cup sugar
2 eggs
2 tsps vanilla
1 1/4 cups all-purpose flour
1/2 tsp baking soda
1 tsp salt
3 cups quick-cooking oats
1 cup walnuts, chopped
1 cup semisweet chocolate chips

n large bowl cream together butter, brown sugar, and sugar. Beat in eggs one at a time; stir in vanilla. In medium mixing bowl sift together flour, baking soda, and salt; stir into creamed mixture until just blended. Fold in oats, walnuts, and chocolate chips. Drop by teaspoonfuls onto ungreased baking sheets. Bake at 325 degrees 12 minutes.

makes about 3 dozen

chocolate press cookies

makes about 4 dozen

1 1/2 cups butter
1 cup sugar
2 squares (2 oz.) unsweetened chocolate, melted
1 egg
1 tsp vanilla
1/2 tsp almond extract
4 cups all-purpose flour
1 tsp baking powder

I n medium mixing bowl cream together butter and sugar. Beat in chocolate, egg, vanilla, and almond extract; beat well. In small mixing bowl sift together flour and baking powder; stir into creamed mixture, blending well. Force dough through cookie press into desired shapes directly onto ungreased baking sheets. Bake at 400 degrees 8 to 10 minutes.

jamboree cookies

3 cups all-purpose flour
1/2 tsp salt
1 1/4 cups butter
1 cup sugar
2 eggs
2 tbsps vanilla
apricot jam or marmalade
1/3 cup walnuts, finely chopped

in small mixing bowl sift together flour and salt. In medium mixing bowl cream together butter and sugar. Mix in eggs and vanilla; beat well. Mix in dry ingredients. Using tablespoon roll dough into balls and place onto un-greased baking sheets. Use palm of your hand to press each cookie flat. Spoon 1/4 teaspoon apricot jam into center of cookie. Sprinkle with chopped walnuts. Bake at 375 degrees 8 to 10 minutes.

makes 7 to 8 dozen

peanutty pick-me-ups

3/4 cup butter
1/2 cup powdered sugar, sifted
1/4 cup brown sugar, firmly packed
1 tsp vanilla
2 cups all-purpose flour
1 cup salted peanuts, chopped

n medium mixing bowl cream together butter, powdered sugar, brown sugar, and vanilla. Thoroughly blend in flour and stir in peanuts. Refrigerate dough for easier handling (one hour or until firm). Form dough into logs about 3 inches long and 1/2 inch diameter. Put on ungreased cookie sheet and lightly flatten. Bake at 350 degrees 12 to 15 minutes.

makes about 5 dozen

raisin rounds

makes about 6 dozen

4 cups all-purpose flour, sifted
1 tsp baking soda
1 tsp salt
1 tbsp orange rind, grated
3 cups (15 oz.) seedless raisins
3/4 cup sugar
3/4 cup brown sugar, firmly packed
1 cup shortening
1 egg
2/3 cup sour cream
1 tsp vanilla

In medium mixing bowl sift together flour, baking soda, and salt. Stir in orange rind and raisins; set aside. Cream together sugar, brown sugar, and shortening. Beat in egg and half the flour mixture; stir well. Mix in sour cream, vanilla, and remaining flour mixture; blend well. Refrigerate dough for easier handling (one hour or until firm). Using teaspoon form dough into balls. Put on ungreased baking sheets. Using fork flatten each ball to 1/8- to 1/4-inch thick. Bake at 375 degrees 10 to 13 minutes.

honey peanut cookies

2 3/4 cups all-purpose flour, sifted
2 tsps baking powder
1/4 tsp salt
3/4 cup butter
1 cup sugar
2 eggs
1 tsp vanilla
filling (see below)

in small mixing bowl sift together flour, baking powder, and salt. In separate bowl, cream together butter and sugar. Beat in eggs and vanilla; mix well. Stir in flour mixture; blend well. Refrigerate dough 1 hour. On floured surface roll 1/3 of dough to 1/8-inch thick. Cut into an even number of circles 2 1/2 inches in diameter and place half on ungreased cookie sheet. Place teaspoonful of filling in center of each circle. Top each with another circle and seal edges. Bake at 400 degrees 8 to 10 minutes.

filling

1 cup raisins, finely chopped
1/3 cup peanuts, finely chopped
2 tbsps butter, softened
1/3 cup honey
1/2 tsp cinnamon

To make filling:
In small mixing bowl mix together all ingredients.

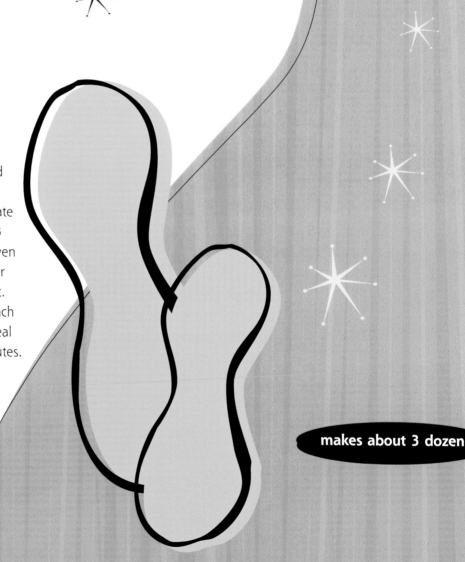

makes about 3 dozen

harvest spice pressed cookies

2 cups all-purpose flour
1 tsp ginger
1 tsp cloves
1 tsp cinnamon
1/2 tsp baking soda
1/2 tsp salt
3/4 cup sugar
3/4 cup shortening
1 egg
3 tbsps molasses
1 tsp lemon extract

 n small bowl sift together flour, ginger, cloves, cinnamon, baking soda, and salt; set aside. Cream together sugar and shortening. Beat in egg, molasses, and lemon extract; mix well. Gradually stir in dry ingredients; blend thoroughly. Using cookie press with tooth plate, press dough into long strips across ungreased cookie sheets. Bake at 375 degrees 5 to 7 minutes; cool 1 minute. Carefully cut into 2 1/2-inch strips and remove.

makes about 8 dozen

In the late 1940s, as the postwar boom began, a new sense of prosperity appeared on street corners, in shops, and in American homes. Rationing was out, fanciful was in! Homemakers were no exception, and they took pride in creating foods that accentuated their newfound affluence. No longer was chocolate cake enough. Rich Red Velvet cake was born as cooks dressed up Devil's Food cake to give it a dark red hue and a dashing, dramatic look. It was served in homes everywhere.

Home cooks also looked for new ways to create their cakes. In 1948 both Pillsbury and General Mills introduced their first boxed cake mixes to consumers. The 1950s brought a variety of flavored cake mixes to homemakers, which gave them more tools to streamline preparation. They simply had to add a few ingredients (eggs, oil, and water) and stir, and the cake was ready to bake. Time-consuming angel food cake became simple to make with a mix.

Cakes took on a special meaning for me when, early in my career, I had the opportunity to judge entries in the cakes category at the Iowa State Fair. With great joy I accepted the assignment. Those proud cooks were the best Iowa had to offer. From small rural communities and large urban areas, they baked and frosted and glazed again and again, all hoping to come home with blue ribbons. They had honed their skills on cake after cake using real butter, cream, and fresh eggs, creating cakes that were nothing short of miraculous. We judges sat in front of rows of homemade moist, pungent spice cakes; rich chocolate cakes with creamy frostings swirled between layers and on top; feathery, delicate angel food cakes; and citrus-spiked chiffon cakes. We looked, we tasted, we compared. Although only a few cakes won the coveted blue ribbons, all were winners.

It is that excellence and pride of being a blue-ribbon baker, whether at a fair or in the kitchen, that cooks strive for. You'll find the cakes in this chapter deliciously sweet and all worthy of a most-prized blue ribbon.

Poppy seed cake

1/3 cup poppy seeds
1/2 cup milk
2 cups all-purpose flour
3 tsps baking powder
1 tsp salt
3 egg whites (reserve 2 yolks for filling)
1 1/4 cups sugar
1/3 cup shortening
1/2 cup heavy cream
1 tsp vanilla
sprinkling of powdered sugar
filling (see below)
topping (see below)

makes 2 layers

Grease and flour two 8-inch round cake pans. In small bowl or cup, soak poppy seeds in milk. In small mixing bowl sift together flour, baking powder, and salt. In medium mixing bowl beat egg whites until stiff and still moist. In another bowl cream together sugar and shortening. Add vanilla to cream and add to sugar-shortening mixture, alternating with dry ingredients; mix well after each addition. Stir in poppy seed-milk mixture. Carefully fold in egg whites until thoroughly mixed. Pour into cake pans and bake at 375 degrees 25 to 30 minutes. Remove from pans and cool. Spread filling between layers and sprinkle top with powdered sugar.

filling

1 1/2 cups milk, divided
2 tbsps butter
1/3 cup all-purpose flour
1/3 cup sugar
1/4 tsp salt
2 egg yolks, slightly beaten
1 tsp vanilla

To make filling:

In medium saucepan heat 1 cup milk and butter. In small mixing bowl blend together flour, sugar, and salt. Add remaining 1/2 cup milk; stir well. Add mixture to hot milk-butter mixture and cook over medium heat until thick, stirring constantly. Blend a little of hot mixture into egg yolks and then add yolks to hot mixture. Continue cooking approximately 2 more minutes, stirring constantly. Cool, then add vanilla; mix thoroughly.

spice cake

1 1/4 cups
  sugar, divided
2 tsps cinnamon
3 tbsps water
1 3/4 cups all-purpose flour, sifted
2 tsps baking powder
1/2 tsp salt
1/3 cup butter
2/3 cup milk
1 tsp vanilla
2 egg whites
topping (see below)

grease and flour bottom of 9 x 9 x 2-inch square pan. In small saucepan combine 1/4 cup sugar, cinnamon, and water. Stir constantly and cook until mixture begins to boil. Remove from heat and set aside. In small bowl sift together flour, baking powder, and salt. In medium mixing bowl cream together butter and remaining cup of sugar. Mix together milk and vanilla. Add to creamed mixture alternating with dry ingredients, blending well after each addition. Beat egg whites until stiff and still moist; gently fold into batter. Pour into pan and drizzle cinnamon-water syrup over top. Cut through batter randomly with knife to create marbled effect. Bake at 350 degrees 35 to 40 minutes. Serve with topping.

makes 1 cake

topping

3/4 cup whipping cream
3 tbsps sugar
1/2 tsp vanilla
1/4 tsp cinnamon

To make topping:

In small mixing bowl beat whipping cream until thick. Stir in sugar, vanilla, and cinnamon.

lemon tea cake

1/2 cup golden raisins, chopped
1 1/2 tsps lemon rind, grated
2/3 cup hot strong black tea
1 3/4 cups all-purpose flour
1 tsp salt
3/4 tsp baking soda
1 cup sugar
1/2 cup shortening
2 eggs
frosting (see below)

makes 1 cake

frosting

1/4 cup butter
2 tbsps milk
1 tsp lemon rind, grated
1 tbsp lemon juice
1/3 tsp vanilla
1/8 tsp salt
2 cups powdered sugar

Grease and flour bottom of 9 x 9 x 2-inch square pan. In small bowl combine raisins, lemon rind, and tea. Cool and then drain, reserving liquid. In medium mixing bowl sift together flour, salt, and baking soda; stir in drained raisins and set aside. Cream together sugar and shortening. Add eggs and beat well. Add dry ingredients alternately with reserved liquid, blending well after each addition. Pour into pan and bake at 350 degrees 40 to 45 minutes. Cool before frosting.

To make frosting:
In small mixing bowl cream butter. Blend in milk, lemon rind, lemon juice, vanilla, and salt. Beat in powdered sugar until smooth. If necessary, thin with milk.

72

fluffy buttermilk cake

grease and flour two round cake pans. In small bowl sift together flour, salt, and baking soda. In another small bowl beat egg yolks approximately 5 minutes or until thick and lemon colored; set aside. Cream together sugar and shortening; blend in yolks. Mix together buttermilk, vanilla, and lemon rind. Add to creamed mixture alternately with dry ingredients, blending well after each addition. Pour into cake pans and bake at 350 degrees 30 to 35 minutes. Cool before frosting.

1 3/4 cups all-purpose flour
1 tsp salt
1/2 tsp baking soda
8 egg yolks (approximately 2/3 cup)
   (reserve 2 egg whites for frosting)
1 1/4 cups sugar
1/2 cup shortening
3/4 cup buttermilk
1/2 tsp vanilla
1 tsp lemon rind, grated
frosting (see right)

frosting

3/4 cup sugar
1/4 cup light corn syrup
2 egg whites
2 tbsps orange juice
1 tsp orange rind, grated
1/4 tsp salt
1/4 tsp cream of tartar

To make frosting:
In top of double boiler, beat together all ingredients. Cook over rapidly boiling water, beating with electric mixer or rotary beater until mixture stands in peaks. Remove from heat and continue beating until smooth and spreadable.

makes 2 layers

perfect chocolate cake

2 cups all-purpose flour
3 tsps baking powder
1/2 tsp salt
1 cup sugar
1/2 cup shortening
3 eggs, separated (reserve whites)
1 cup milk
1 tsp vanilla
3 squares (3 oz.) semisweet
    chocolate, coarsely grated
frosting (see right)

frosting

1/3 cup (3 oz.) cream cheese
3 tbsps milk
1/8 tsp salt
2 1/2 cups powdered sugar
2 squares (2 oz.) unsweetened chocolate, melted
1 tsp vanilla

grease and flour bottoms of two round cake pans. In small bowl sift together flour, baking powder, and salt. In medium mixing bowl cream together sugar and shortening. Beat in egg yolks. Mix together milk and vanilla. Alternately add to creamed mixture with dry ingredients, blending well after each addition. Fold in chocolate. In small mixing bowl beat egg whites until stiff and still moist; fold gently into batter. Pour into pans and bake at 350 degrees 30 to 35 minutes. Cool before frosting.

To make frosting:
In small mixing bowl blend cream cheese, milk, and salt. Slowly add powdered sugar, beating well. Add chocolate and vanilla; continue beating until smooth and spreadable. If necessary, thin with milk.

makes 2 layers

dreamy cream cake

2 cups all-purpose flour
2 tsps baking powder
1 tsp salt
1/2 cup butter
1 cup sugar
1 egg
2 egg yolks (reserve whites
   for meringue)
1 cup milk
1 tsp vanilla
filling (see right)
meringue (see right)

grease and flour bottoms of two 8-inch round cake pans. In small bowl sift together flour, baking powder, and salt. In medium mixing bowl cream together butter and sugar. Beat in egg and egg yolks; mix well. Combine milk and vanilla and alternately add to creamed mixture with dry ingredients, blending well after each addition. Pour into cake pans and bake at 350 degrees 25 to 30 minutes. Cool and place on ovenproof plate. Spread filling between layers and spread meringue on top and sides. Bake at 350 degrees another 10 to 15 minutes.

filling

1 cup milk, divided
2 tbsps butter
1/3 cup sugar
2 tbsps all-purpose flour
1/4 tsp salt
1 egg, slightly beaten
1/2 tsp vanilla

To make filling:
In saucepan heat 2/3 cup milk and butter. In small mixing bowl combine sugar, flour, and salt. Mix in remaining 1/3 cup milk and stir until smooth. Add to hot milk mixture and cook over medium heat until thick, stirring constantly. Blend small amount of hot mixture with egg. Add back to hot mixture and cook another 2 minutes, stirring constantly. Cool before stirring in vanilla.

makes 2 layers

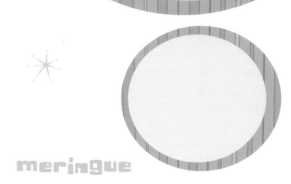

meringue

3 egg whites
6 tbsps sugar
1/2 tsp vanilla

To make meringue:
In small mixing bowl beat egg whites until soft mounds form. Slowly add sugar while continuing to beat; blend well. Mix in vanilla and keep beating until meringue stands in stiff, glossy peaks.

75

coconut cake

3 cups all-purpose flour
3 tsps baking powder
1 tsp salt
2 cups sugar
1 cup shortening
4 eggs
1 cup milk
1 tsp vanilla
1 cup coconut, shredded
frosting (see below)

Grease and flour bottoms of three round cake pans. In small bowl sift together flour, baking powder, and salt. Cream together sugar and shortening. Beat in eggs, one at a time. Combine milk and vanilla and add to creamed mixture alternately with dry ingredients, blending well after each addition. Fold in coconut and pour batter into pans. Bake at 350 degrees 25 to 30 minutes. Cool before frosting.

frosting

1 cup sugar
1/2 cup light corn syrup
3 egg whites
3 tbsps water
1/4 tsp salt
1/4 tsp cream of tartar
1 1/2 tsps vanilla

makes 3 layers

To make frosting:
In top of double boiler, combine all ingredients except vanilla. Cook over rapidly boiling water, beating with electric mixer or rotary beater until mixture stands in peaks. Remove from heat and add vanilla. Continue beating until spreadable.

black walnut cake

2 cups all-purpose flour
3 tsps baking powder
1/2 tsp baking soda
1/2 tsp salt
3 tbsps butter, softened
1 cup plus 2 tbsps sugar
1 1/2 cups sour cream
1/4 tsp black walnut flavoring
2 eggs
frosting (see below)

Grease and flour bottom of 12 x 8 x 2-inch rectangle pan. In mixing bowl sift together flour, baking powder, baking soda, and salt. Cream together butter and sugar. Mix in sour cream and black walnut flavoring. Beat in eggs one at a time. Add dry ingredients and mix thoroughly. Pour into pan and bake at 350 degrees 45 to 50 minutes. Cool before frosting.

frosting

1/4 cup butter
1/2 cup brown sugar, firmly packed
1/4 cup cream
1 1/2 cups powdered sugar, sifted
1/3 cups nuts, chopped (optional)
1/2 tsp vanilla

makes 1 cake

To make frosting:

In small saucepan melt butter; add brown sugar and cook over medium heat 2 minutes, stirring constantly. Blend in cream and continue stirring while bringing to a boil. Remove from heat and mix in sugar and nuts, if using; stir well. Beat in vanilla until spreadable. If necessary, thin with milk.

easy tea time cake

2 cups all-purpose flour
1/2 tsp baking powder
3/4 cup butter
1/3 cup (3 oz.) cream cheese
1 1/2 cups sugar
5 eggs

makes 1 cake

Grease bottom of 9-inch tube pan. In small bowl sift together flour and baking powder. Cream together butter and cream cheese. Gradually add sugar; beat well. Add eggs one at a time, beating well after each. Stir in dry ingredients until thoroughly blended. Pour into pan and bake at 350 degrees 30 minutes. Reduce oven temperature to 300 degrees and bake an additional 40 to 50 minutes.

yellow pound cake

2 1/4 cups all-purpose flour
2 tsps baking powder
1/2 tsp salt
9 egg yolks
1/2 cup butter
1 1/2 cups sugar
1 cup milk
1 tsp lemon extract
frosting (see below)

Grease and flour bottom of 9-inch tube pan. In small bowl sift together flour, baking powder, and salt. Beat egg yolks until thick, approximately 5 minutes. Cream together butter and sugar; beat in egg yolks. Combine milk and lemon extract and add to creamed mixture alternately with dry ingredients, blending well after each addition. Pour into pan and bake at 325 degrees 50 to 60 minutes. Cool before frosting. (Note: Cake is also wonderful without frosting.)

frosting

1/4 cup butter
2 tbsps milk
1 tsp lemon rind, grated
1 tbsp lemon juice
1/4 tsp vanilla
dash of salt
2 cups powdered sugar

To make frosting:

Cream together all ingredients and beat until smooth and spreadable. If necessary, thin with milk.

makes 1 cake

speedy orange nut cake

2 1/4 cups all-purpose flour
1 1/2 cups sugar
3 tsps baking powder
1 tsp salt
1/2 cup shortening
3/4 cup nuts, chopped and divided
3 eggs
1 cup milk
1 tsp vanilla
1 orange rind, grated

grease and flour bottom of 12 x 8 x 2-inch pan. In small bowl sift together flour, sugar, baking powder, and salt. Beat in shortening, 1/2 cup nuts, eggs, milk, vanilla, and orange rind. Continue beating for approximately 2 to 3 minutes. Pour into pan and sprinkle with remaining 1/4 cup nuts. Bake at 350 degrees 45 to 55 minutes.

makes 1 cake

WHOOSH

devil's food cake

3/4 cup milk
1 tbsp vinegar
1 3/4 cups all-purpose flour
1/2 tsp salt
1 1/2 cups sugar
1/2 cup shortening
2 eggs
1 tsp vanilla
1 tsp baking soda
1/2 cup cocoa
1/2 cup warm water
frosting (see right)

makes 2 layers

frosting

3 1/2 cups powdered sugar
1/3 cup cocoa
1/8 tsp salt
1/3 cup butter
1 egg
1 tsp vanilla
4 to 5 tbsps hot cream

To make frosting:

In small bowl sift together sugar, cocoa, and salt. Cream together butter, egg, and vanilla. Alternately add dry ingredients and hot cream. Beat well until spreadable.

 rease and flour bottoms of two round cake pans. Mix together milk and vinegar. In small bowl sift together flour and salt. Cream together sugar and shortening. Add eggs one at a time; beat well. Stir vanilla into milk mixture. Add to creamed mixture alternately with dry ingredients, mixing well after each addition. Mix together baking soda, cocoa, and water; add to batter, mixing well. Pour into pans and bake at 350 degrees 30 to 35 minutes. Cool before frosting.

traditional sponge cake

1 cup all-purpose flour
1 tsp baking powder
1/4 tsp salt
2 eggs
1 cup sugar
1 tsp vanilla
1/2 cup scalded milk
frosting (see right)

Grease and flour bottom of 8 x 8 x 2-inch square pan. In small bowl sift together flour, baking powder, and salt. Beat eggs until thick; add sugar slowly while still beating. Quickly mix in dry ingredients; add vanilla and milk. Mix quickly and thoroughly. Pour into pan and bake at 350 degrees 30 to 35 minutes. Cool before frosting.

makes 1 cake

frosting

1/4 cup butter, melted
1/2 cup brown sugar, firmly packed
3 tbsps cream
1 cup coconut, shredded

To make frosting:
In medium mixing bowl combine butter, brown sugar, cream, and coconut; mix well. Place cake on ovenproof plate and frost. Broil 1 to 3 minutes or until golden brown – watch closely!

apple-coffee cake

1 1/2 cups all-purpose flour, divided
1 cup less 2 tbsps sugar
1 tsp salt
1 tsp cinnamon
1/4 tsp ground cloves
1 cup (1 medium) apple, peeled and finely chopped
1/2 cup raisins
1/2 cup shortening
2 eggs
1 tsp baking soda
1/2 cup cold coffee
frosting (see below)

Grease and flour bottom of 9 x 9 x 2-inch square pan. In small bowl sift together 1 1/4 cups flour, sugar, salt, cinnamon, and cloves. Stir together apple, raisins, and remaining 1/4 cup flour. In medium mixing bowl cream shortening. Add eggs one at a time and beat well after each. Add baking soda to coffee and stir. Add to shortening mixture alternately with dry ingredients; stir well. Add fruit and mix thoroughly. Pour into pan and bake at 375 degrees 30 to 40 minutes. Cool before frosting.

frosting

3 tbsps butter
1/4 tsp salt
1/2 tsp vanilla
1 1/2 cups powdered sugar, sifted
1 1/2 to 2 tbsps hot coffee

To make frosting:
Cream together butter, salt, and vanilla. Alternately add sugar and coffee and beat until spreadable.

makes 1 cake

chocolate pocket cake

2 1/2 cups all-purpose flour
3 tsps baking powder
1 tsp salt
1 2/3 cups sugar
2/3 cup shortening
3 eggs
1 1/4 cups milk
1/2 tsp vanilla
1 tbsp instant coffee
1 1/2 tbsps cocoa
1 tbsp water
1/4 tsp almond extract
frosting (see below)

makes 4 layers

grease and flour bottom of two round cake pans. In small bowl sift together flour, baking powder, and salt. Cream together sugar and shortening. Add eggs one at a time, beating well after each. Mix together milk and vanilla. Add to creamed mixture alternately with dry ingredients; mix thoroughly. Pour half of batter into one pan. To remaining batter add coffee, cocoa, water, and almond extract. Mix well and pour into second pan. Bake at 350 degrees 30 to 40 minutes. When cake is cool, cut layers in half horizontally, creating four layers. Frost, alternating placing dark and light layers.

frosting

2 cups (12 oz.) semisweet chocolate pieces
1/2 cup butter
1 cup powdered sugar, sifted
3 eggs
1 tsp vanilla

To make frosting:

In top of double boiler, melt chocolate over hot water. Cool to room temperature. In medium mixing bowl cream together butter and sugar. Add eggs one at a time, beating well after each. Add vanilla and melted chocolate; beat until spreadable.

2 cups brown sugar, firmly packed
1/4 cup butter
2 tbsps water
1 1/4 tsps salt, divided
1 cup evaporated milk, undiluted
2 tsps vanilla
2 1/4 cups all-purpose flour
1 tsp baking powder
1 tsp baking soda
1/2 cup shortening
1/2 cup milk
3 eggs
frosting (see below)

old-fashioned caramel cake

makes 2 layers

Grease and flour bottoms of two round cake pans. To make caramel sauce, in medium saucepan mix together brown sugar, butter, water, and 1/4 teaspoon salt. Stirring constantly, cook over medium heat (234 degrees) until soft ball stage. Remove from heat and stir in evaporated milk and vanilla; cool. In large mixing bowl sift together flour, baking powder, baking soda, and remaining teaspoon of salt. Blend in shortening, milk, and 2 cups caramel sauce, reserving the rest for frosting. Beat thoroughly approximately 2 minutes. Add eggs and continue beating another 2 minutes. Pour into pans and bake at 350 degrees 35 to 40 minutes. Cool before frosting.

frosting

reserved caramel sauce
1/3 cup (3 oz.) cream cheese, softened
3 cups powdered sugar
1 tsp vanilla

To make frosting:

In medium mixing bowl cream together reserved caramel sauce and cream cheese. Slowly add sugar and vanilla; beat well. If necessary, thin with milk.

yummy hunny cake

2 **1/2** cups all-purpose flour
2 tsps baking powder
1 tsp cinnamon
1 tsp mace
1/2 tsp salt
1/4 tsp baking soda
3/4 cup sugar
1/2 cup shortening
1 tsp orange rind, grated
2/3 cup milk
2/3 cup honey, divided
1 tsp vanilla
2 eggs
1/2 cup pecans, chopped

rease and flour bottom of 12 x 8 x 2-inch rectangle pan. In small bowl sift together flour, baking powder, cinnamon, mace, salt, and baking soda. Cream together sugar, shortening, and orange rind. Cut in dry ingredients until crumbly. Remove 3/4 cup for topping and set aside. To remaining crumb mixture stir in milk, 1/2 cup honey, and vanilla; beat well for approximately 2 minutes. Add eggs and beat 1 more minute. Pour into pan. Mix together reserved crumb mixture, pecans, and remaining honey; sprinkle over batter. Bake at 350 degrees 35 to 45 minutes.

2 cups all-purpose
  flour, sifted
1 1/4 cups sugar
2 tsps baking powder
1 tsp salt
2 tsps instant coffee

1 cup milk, divided
1/2 cup shortening
3 tbsps molasses
2 eggs
1 tsp vanilla
frosting (see right)
topping (see right)

Grease and flour bottom of 12 x 8 x 2-inch rectangle pan. In large mixing bowl sift together flour, sugar, baking powder, and salt; stir in coffee. Add 3/4 cup milk, shortening, and molasses; beat well. Add remaining 1/4 cup milk, eggs, and vanilla. Beat 2 minutes. Pour into pan and bake at 350 degrees 35 to 45 minutes. Cool before frosting; sprinkle topping on frosting.

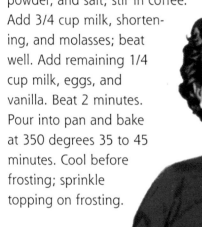

frosting

1/3 cup all-purpose flour
2/3 cup sugar
2 tbsps cornstarch
2 1/4 cups cold milk
3 egg yolks, slightly beaten
2 tsps vanilla
3/4 cup butter, creamed

To make frosting:

In medium saucepan combine flour, sugar, and cornstarch. Stirring constantly, add milk and cook until thick. Mix a little of hot mixture into egg yolks; add yolks back into hot mixture. Cook over low heat 2 minutes, stirring constantly. Mix in vanilla, then cover; cool. Stir in butter when mixture reaches lukewarm. Cool completely before frosting.

topping

1/4 cup all-purpose flour
2 tbsps brown sugar
2 tbsps butter
1/4 cup pecans, chopped

To make topping:

In small mixing bowl mix together flour and brown sugar. Cut in butter until crumbly; add pecans. Place in small pan and bake at 350 degrees 15 minutes. Cool completely, then break into small pieces and sprinkle over frosting.

makes 1 cake

burnt sugar cake

1 1/2 cups sugar, divided
1/2 cup boiling water
1/4 to 1/3 cup milk
2 cups all-purpose flour
3 tbsps double-acting baking
    powder
1 tsp salt
1/2 cup shortening
2 eggs
1 tsp vanilla
frosting (see right)

Grease and flour bottoms of two round cake pans. In heavy skillet cook 3/4 cup sugar over low heat until medium to dark brown, stirring constantly. Add boiling water, a few drops at a time. Stir well after each addition until sugar dissolves. Set aside and cool. Reserving 2 tablespoons sugar syrup for frosting, pour remainder into measuring cup and add enough milk to measure 1 cup. In large mixing bowl sift together flour, remaining 3/4 cup sugar, baking powder, and salt. Beat in shortening and syrup-milk mixture. Add eggs and vanilla; beat 2 minutes. Pour into pans and bake at 350 degrees 30 to 35 minutes. Cool before frosting.

frosting

3/4 cup sugar
2 tbsps light corn syrup
2 tbsps reserved sugar syrup
2 egg whites
2 tbsps water
1/4 tsp salt
1/4 tsp cream of tartar
1 tsp vanilla

makes 2 layers

To make frosting:
In top of double boiler, mix together sugar, corn syrup, sugar syrup, egg whites, water, salt, and cream of tartar. Beat mixture while cooking over rapidly boiling water. Beat until mixture forms peaks; remove from heat, add vanilla, and continue beating until spreadable.

grandma's brown bear cake

1 2/3 cups all-purpose flour
2 tsps baking powder
1 tsp salt
1/2 tsp cinnamon
1/4 tsp allspice
10 egg yolks
1/2 cup butter
1 cup sugar
1/2 cup milk
1 tsp vanilla
1 square (1 oz.) semi-sweet or unsweetened chocolate, grated
frosting (see below)

makes 2 layers

Preheat oven to 325 degrees. Grease and flour two 8-inch round cake pans. In a mixing bowl sift together flour, baking powder, salt, cinnamon, and allspice. In a small mixing bowl beat egg yolks until thick. Cream together butter and sugar, beat well. Add the egg yolks and mix well. Alternately add milk and vanilla with the dry ingredients to the creamed mixture, blending well after each addition. Fold in chocolate. Pour batter into cake pans. Bake for 25 to 30 minutes or until an inserted toothpick comes out clean. Cool and frost.

1 cup sugar
1 cup brown sugar, firmly packed
2/3 cup sour cream
1 tsp vanilla

To make frosting:

In a saucepan blend together sugars and sour cream. Heat to softball stage (236 degrees). Remove from heat and cool until slightly warm. Beat in vanilla until it reaches spreading consistency. Thin with milk if necessary.

pies

"**A**s American as apple pie." It's a saying that reflects America's ongoing love affair with this dessert favorite. Pie has long been the center of contests and competitions. From auctioneers seeking bidders in pie-supper auctions to county and state fair contests, 4-H youth contests, and national pie-baking contests, pie in all its forms is a dessert worthy of distinction and honor. The American Pie Council has even created National Pie Day (January 23) to honor pie.

Pies have always been the crowning glory of potlucks, parties, and social gatherings. More than a century ago families feasted on plump fruit pies packed with local fruit and sometimes even vegetables. Lard was used to create the most tender and flaky of pie crusts. Diners oohed and ahhed – a sign of appreciation and admiration for the cook. Orchard-fresh apple, peach, and berry pies were often the most requested desserts and were always a hit with contest judges as well as with family and friends.

As time passed, however, homemakers began to think about easier and lighter ways to enjoy pie. They were eager to put on their aprons and roll up their sleeves as they began creating "new" pies to add to the most requested list. These pies did without the pastry, and the crusts were made with graham cracker or cookie crumbs. Fillings were creamy, light, and airy. Lemon Chiffon Pie, French Silk Pie, and various ice cream pies were the new taste sensations. With Frank Sinatra, Dean Martin, and other Rat Pack crooners fashionably in vogue, sipping their drinks and singing late into the night, cooks took their lead and infused pies with colorful, tasty liqueurs that gave us Grasshopper Pie and Brandy Alexander Pie.

Even though pie has evolved into one of the most popular of desserts in all its various forms, traditional homemade pie is still a real treat. Take a trip down memory lane with these recipes and discover why pie is all the rage. These rich cream pies and succulent fruit pies will have you asking, "Another piece of pie?"

apple crumble pie

one-crust pastry (see page 41)
1/2 cup sugar
1/4 cup plus 1 tbsp all-purpose flour, divided
1/4 tsp salt
1 egg, slightly beaten
3/4 cup sour cream
1 tsp vanilla
2 cups (2 medium) apples, peeled, cored, and chopped
1/4 cup brown sugar, firmly packed
2 tbsps butter

Prepare recipe for one-crust pastry (do not prick crust). In medium mixing bowl blend together sugar, 1 tablespoon flour, and salt. Stir in egg, sour cream, vanilla, and apples. Pour into pie shell and bake at 450 degrees 10 minutes. In small bowl stir together remaining 1/4 cup flour and brown sugar. Using fork cut in butter until crumbly. Sprinkle over pie and reduce oven temperature to 350 degrees. Bake an additional 25 to 30 minutes until custard is set.

makes 1 pie

rosy apple pie

Now... in midwinter
Orchard-fresh slices
– that bake into the most luscious apple pies ever!

Comstock
PIE-SLICED APPLES

two-crust pastry (see right)

5 cups (5 medium) apples, peeled, cored, and sliced (reserve peelings)

1/2 cup water

1 to 2 drops red food coloring

1 cup sugar

2 tbsps all-purpose flour

1 tsp lemon rind, grated

1 tbsp lemon juice

1/4 tsp nutmeg

1 tbsp butter

makes 1 pie

Prepare recipe for two-crust pastry and line pie pan with half of dough. In saucepan combine apple peelings and water. Cover and cook about 10 minutes to make juice. Add red food coloring. Mix together sugar and flour. Sprinkle half of mixture into bottom of pie shell. In medium mixing bowl stir together apple slices, lemon rind, lemon juice, and nutmeg. Layer apple mixture in pie shell and sprinkle sugar mixture over each layer. Pour 3 tablespoons apple peeling juice over pie filling and dot with butter. Using fingers or pastry brush, dampen rim of bottom crust, then lay top crust over filling. Pinch edges of crusts together and flute. Cut slits in top crust for steam vents. Bake at 450 degrees 10 minutes. Reduce oven temperature to 375 degrees and bake an additional 40 to 50 minutes.

two crust pastry

2 cups flour

1 tsp salt

2/3 cup butter or shortening

one glass ice water

To make pastry:

Mix flour and salt in medium mixing bowl. Use pastry cutter to blend in butter or shortening until mixture becomes crumbly. Add 5 to 6 table-spoons of ice water one at a time until dough is moist enough to stick together. Divide and form into two balls. Flatten one ball to 1/2-inch thickness, smooth rough edges, and roll out onto floured surface. Dough should form even circle 1 1/2 inches larger than an 8- or 9-inch pie pan. Place crust loosely in pan, pat out air pockets, and add filling. Roll out second ball of dough with same method as the first and top pie as instructed.

blueberry cream pie

one-crust pastry
(see page 41)
3/4 cup sugar
2 1/2 tbsps cornstarch
1/4 tsp salt
2/3 cup water
3 cups blueberries,
    fresh or frozen, divided
2 tbsps butter
1 1/2 tbsps lemon juice
1 cup whipping cream
1 tbsp powdered sugar
1/2 tsp vanilla

makes 1 pie

Prepare recipe for one-crust pastry and bake as directed. In saucepan blend together sugar, cornstarch, and salt. Stir in water and 1 cup blueberries. Stirring constantly, bring to boil and cook until very thick. Add butter and lemon juice; mix well and let cool. Gently stir in remaining 2 cups blueberries and refrigerate about 1 hour. In small mixing bowl beat whipping cream until thick. Mix in powdered sugar and vanilla. Cover bottom of pie shell with half the whipped cream. Pour blueberry filling over whipped cream. Chill about 2 hours. Top pie with remaining whipped cream.

cherry cheesecake pie

1/2 cup butter
2 tbsps sugar
1/8 tsp salt
1 cup all-purpose flour, sifted
cherry filling (see below)
topping (see below)

n small mixing bowl cream together all ingredients. Blend in flour and press mixture into bottom and sides of pie pan (not on rim).

opping

/3 cup (6 oz.) cream cheese, softened
egg
/3 cup sugar
/2 tsp vanilla

o make topping:
eat together all ingredients
ntil thick and creamy.

cherry filling

1 No. 2 can (20 oz.) sour pie cherries
1/2 cup sugar
3 tbsps all-purpose flour

To make filling:
Drain cherries, reserving juice (approximately 3/4 cup); set aside. In small saucepan mix together sugar, flour, and cherry juice; blend well. Stirring constantly, cook over medium heat until thickened. Remove from heat and add cherries. Pour into pie shell and bake at 350 degrees 15 minutes. Spread topping around filling to edge of the crust, leaving a 2- to 3-inch uncovered circle in center of pie. Return to oven and bake an additional 30 minutes.

makes 1 pie

tropical tangy pie

one-crust pastry (see page 41)
1 cup sugar
1/2 cup all-purpose flour, sifted
1/4 tsp salt
2 to 3 tsps lemon rind, grated
1 1/4 cups water
1/4 to 1/3 cup lemon juice
1 cup (9-oz. can) crushed pineapple
3 egg yolks, slightly beaten
1 tbsp butter
whipped cream for garnish
nuts for garnish

Prepare recipe for one-crust pastry and bake as directed. In saucepan mix together sugar, flour, salt, and lemon rind. Stir in water, lemon juice, and pineapple; mix well. Stirring constantly, bring to boil and cook over medium heat until thick. Stir small amount of hot mixture into egg yolks. Stirring constantly, add yolks to hot mixture and cook an additional 2 minutes. Add butter and stir; cover and cool. Pour into pie shell and top with whipped cream and nuts.

makes 1 pie

fresh pear pie

two-crust pastry (see page 93)
1/2 cup sugar
3 tbsps flour
1 tsp cinnamon
1/4 tsp salt
5 cups (6 to 7) pears, peeled, cored, and sliced
1 tsp lemon rind, grated
1 tbsp lemon juice
1 tbsp butter

Prepare recipe for two-crust pastry and line pie pan with half of dough. In small bowl mix together sugar, flour, cinnamon, and salt. Layer pear slices in pie shell and sprinkle sugar mixture over each layer. Sprinkle lemon rind and lemon juice on top of pears and dot with butter. Using fingers or pastry brush, dampen rim of bottom crust, then lay top crust over filling. Pinch edges of crusts together and flute. Cut slits in top crust for steam vents. Bake at 450 degrees 10 minutes. Reduce oven temperature to 350 degrees and bake an additional 35 to 40 minutes.

makes one pie

golden dream peach pie

one-crust pastry (see page 41)
1/4 tsp nutmeg
12 fresh or canned peach halves
    or 3 cups peach slices, drained
3 tbsps butter
1 cup brown sugar, firmly packed
1/3 cup all-purpose flour
2 tbsps water
2 cups whipping cream
1/2 tsp vanilla

makes 1 pie

Prepare recipe for one-crust pastry as instructed, adding nutmeg to pastry flour. Arrange peaches in pie shell. In small saucepan melt butter. Blend in brown sugar, flour, and water. Heat until sugar melts, reserve 1 tablespoon syrup, and pour remainder over peaches. Bake at 450 degrees 10 minutes. Reduce oven temperature to 375 degrees and bake an additional 25 to 35 minutes. Cool thoroughly. Beat whipping cream until thick. Add vanilla and reserved syrup; mix well. Spread cream mixture around edge of pie.

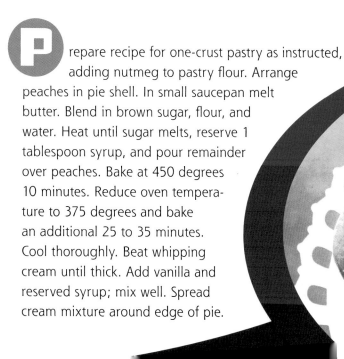

strawberry pie delicious

lattice pastry (see right)
1 cup sugar
1/4 cup cornstarch
1/2 tsp salt
4 cups (1 quart) fresh strawberries, sliced
1/2 cup pineapple tidbits or crushed pineapple, drained
2 tbsps butter

Prepare recipe for lattice pastry. In large mixing bowl stir together sugar, cornstarch, and salt. Fold in strawberries and pineapple. Pour into pie shell and dot with butter. Roll out remaining pastry dough. Cut into 1/2-inch strips and crisscross over filling to form lattice top. Seal ends and flute. Bake at 425 degrees 10 minutes. Reduce oven temperature to 350 degrees and bake an additional 30 to 40 minutes.

lattice pastry

1 1/2 cups all-purpose flour
1/2 tsp salt
1/2 cup shortening
4 to 5 tbsps cold water

To make lattice pastry:
In small mixing bowl sift together flour and salt. Using pastry cutter or fork cut in shortening until dough becomes crumbly. Sprinkle cold water over mixture and lightly stir until dough holds together. Roll two-thirds of dough into circle about 1 inch larger than top rim of pie pan. Carefully lay dough into pan. Reserve remaining one-third dough for lattice top.

makes 1 pie

coconut pie

one-crust pastry (see page 41)
3 eggs, separated (reserve whites)
1 1/4 cups sugar
1 tsp salt
1/2 cup milk
2 tbsps butter, softened
1/2 tsp almond extract
1/4 tsp lemon extract
1 cup coconut, flaked or shredded

Prepare recipe for one-crust pastry. In medium mixing bowl beat egg yolks until thick. Blend in sugar and salt. Stir in milk, butter, and both extracts; beat well. Fold in coconut. In small bowl beat egg whites until stiff but still moist. Gently fold into egg yolk mixture and pour into pie shell. Bake at 350 degrees 35 to 40 minutes.

makes 1 pie

lemon Pie

one-crust pastry (see page 41)
1/2 cup butter
1 1/4 cups sugar
1 tbsp all-purpose flour
3 eggs
1 to 2 tsps lemon rind, grated
1/3 cup lemon juice

Prepare recipe for one-crust pastry. In medium mixing bowl cream together butter and sugar. Mix in flour, stirring well. Beat in eggs one at a time. Add lemon rind and lemon juice; mix well. Pour into pie shell and bake at 400 degrees 10 minutes. Reduce oven temperature to 350 degrees and bake an additional 25 to 30 minutes.

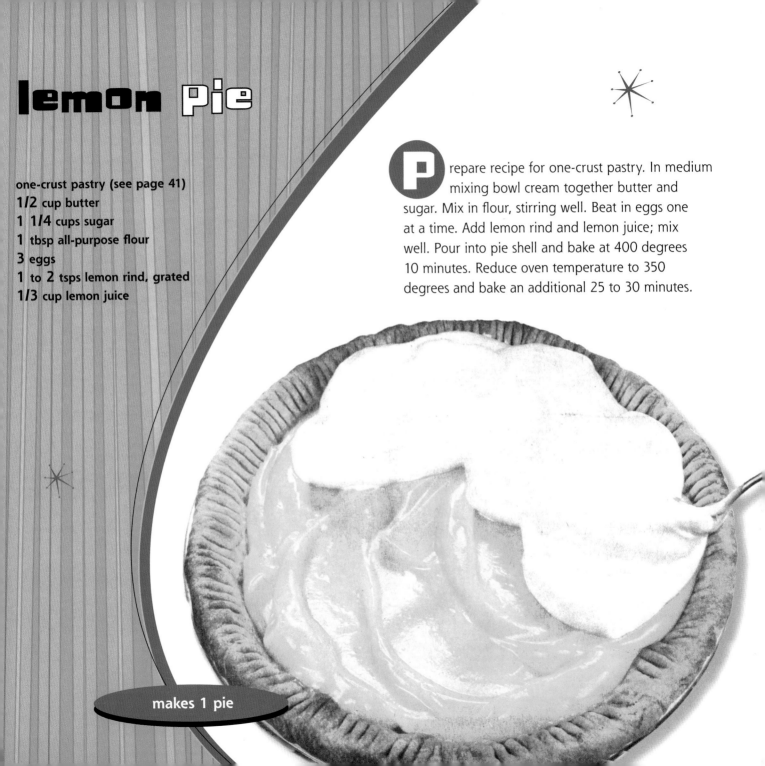

makes 1 pie

spiced pie

one-crust pastry (see page 41)
1/2 cup sugar
2 tbsps flour
1 tsp cinnamon
1/4 tsp nutmeg
1/2 cup apple butter
3 egg yolks, slightly beaten (reserve whites for meringue)
1 cup raisins
3/4 cup evaporated milk, undiluted
1/2 cup water
meringue (see page 75)

Prepare recipe for one-crust pastry. In medium mixing bowl blend together sugar, flour, cinnamon, and nutmeg. Add apple butter, egg yolks, and raisins; mix well. In saucepan mix together evaporated milk and water. Heat until simmering, then add to sugar mixture. Pour into pie shell and bake at 400 degrees 30 to 35 minutes. Spread meringue over filling, reduce oven temperature to 350 degrees, and bake another 12 to15 minutes.

makes 1 pie

chocolate silk pie

[NOTE: This recipe contains raw eggs.]

one-crust pastry (see page 41)
1/2 cup butter
3/4 cup sugar
2 squares (2 oz.) unsweetened chocolate, melted
1 tsp vanilla
2 eggs
whipped cream, for garnish
walnuts, chopped, for garnish

Prepare recipe for one-crust pastry and bake as directed. In medium mixing bowl cream together butter and sugar. Stir in chocolate and vanilla; mix well. Add eggs one at a time, beating a few minutes after each. Pour into pie shell and refrigerate at least 2 hours. Top with whipped cream and walnuts.

makes 1 pie

chocolate peanut pie

1 cup all-purpose flour
1/2 tsp baking powder
1/2 tsp salt
1/3 cup shortening
1/4 cup salted peanuts, crushed
3 to 4 tbsps cold water
filling (see below)

n medium mixing bowl sift together flour, baking powder, and salt. Using pastry cutter or fork cut in shortening until dough becomes crumbly. Stir in peanuts. Sprinkle water over mixture while gently stirring with fork until dough is moist enough to hold together. On floured surface roll dough into circle about 1 inch larger than top rim of pie pan. Gently lay dough into pan and flute; prick all over with fork. Pour in filling and bake at 425 degrees 12 to 15 minutes.

Filling

1 envelope (1 tbsp) unflavored gelatin
1 cup milk, divided
2 squares (2 oz.) unsweetened chocolate
3/4 cup plus 2 tbsps sugar, divided
1/4 tsp salt
1/4 tsp cinnamon
2 eggs, separated (reserve whites)
1/2 tsp vanilla
3/4 cup whipping cream, plus more
    for garnish
peanuts, crushed, for garnish

To make filling:

In small bowl soften gelatin in 1/4 cup milk. In saucepan mix together chocolate, 3/4 cup sugar, salt, cinnamon, and remaining 3/4 cup milk. Stirring constantly, cook over medium heat until mixture is smooth. Mix small amount of hot mixture into beaten egg yolks; add back into hot mixture. Cook another 2 minutes stirring constantly; remove from heat. Stir in vanilla and softened gelatin; mix well until dissolved. Chill until soft set, stirring occasionally. In small mixing bowl beat egg whites until soft mounds form. Slowly add remaining 2 tablespoons sugar and beat until stiff peaks form. Beat whipping cream until thick and fold into beaten egg whites. Fold into gelatin mixture and gently scoop into pie shell. Refrigerate 2 to 3 hours or until set. Top with whipped cream and crushed peanuts.

florida pie

one-crust pastry (see page 41)
1/4 cup walnuts, finely chopped
3/4 cup sugar, divided
1 envelope (1 tbsp) unflavored gelatin
1/8 tsp salt
1 cup cold water
3 eggs, separated (reserve whites)
1/2 cup frozen orange juice, thawed
    and undiluted
whipped cream, for garnish
walnuts, chopped, for garnish

makes 1 pie

Prepare recipe for one-crust pastry, adding 1/4 cup walnuts to pastry flour mixture; bake as directed. In saucepan mix together 1/2 cup sugar, gelatin, salt, and water. Stirring constantly, cook over medium heat until gelatin is dissolved; remove from heat. Beat egg yolks, stir a bit of gelatin mixture into yolks, and add back to gelatin mixture. Stirring constantly, cook over low heat until mixture coats metal spoon, approximately 3 minutes; remove from heat. Add orange juice and chill mixture until soft set. In medium mixing bowl beat egg whites until soft mounds form. Slowly add remaining 1/4 cup sugar and beat until stiff peaks form. Gently fold into gelatin mixture and chill again until thick. Spoon into pie shell and refrigerate until set. Top with whipped cream and walnuts.

southern sugar pie

1 1/2 cups all-purpose flour
1/2 tsp salt
3 tbsps water
1/2 cup shortening
filling (see right)

In medium mixing bowl sift together flour and salt. In another bowl combine water and 1/4 cup of flour mixture. Using pastry cutter or fork cut shortening into remaining flour mixture until dough becomes crumbly. Add flour-water mixture and continue to mix until dough sticks together. On floured surface roll in circle 1 inch larger than top rim of pie pan. Carefully lay into pan and flute. Pour in filling and bake at 350 degrees 45 to 55 minutes.

filling

1 cup sugar
1 cup brown sugar, firmly packed
1/4 cup all-purpose flour, sifted
1/2 tsp salt
4 eggs, beaten until thick
1/2 cup butter, melted
1/2 cup milk
1 tbsp vanilla

To make filling:
In medium mixing bowl mix together sugar, brown sugar, flour, and salt. Beat eggs into dry ingredients; mix thoroughly. Slowly mix in butter, milk, and vanilla.

U AND I SUGAR tops 'em all!*

makes 1 pie

My favorite season in the Midwest is summer. During this warmest time, when days are long and the garden is overflowing with produce, I love to take a tour of our garden and inspect our crop. Our kids run to pick berries, check beans, and keep an eye on the towering corn stalks. Summer is short, though, and all through the year, whenever I need a bit of summer, I head to the kitchen to bake skillet cakes, cobblers, and crisps – old-fashioned comfort desserts.

It was the plentiful native fruits (and vegetables) early settlers found that led them to the creation of cobblers, crisps, and other delicacies. From season to season, homemakers improvised and created sweets using those ingredients available to them. As people moved westward and regional ingredients were introduced, they expanded their repertoire to desserts with citrus fruits and other favorites.

Early bakers also had to contend with temperamental wood or coal cookstoves that demanded special skills to keep the fire the right temperature for baking. By the 1920s, however, many kitchens had gas stoves. Those compact, cleaner stoves gave cooks more control over their cooking, although not necessarily at a cheaper price. Electric stoves and ovens were available at the end of the nineteenth century, but getting electricity to the consumer was a problem. As electricity became more widely available, electric stoves won over consumers with their affordable efficiency and automatic temperature controls. A great challenge to baking had finally been mastered!

When World War II began, cooks were once again forced to improvise. They continued to enthusiastically create fresh, homespun desserts but with new challenges. Rationing limited supplies like sugar, butter, and eggs. Families and friends rallied together to plant Victory Gardens, growing and using their own produce as the war effort continued.

From generation to generation, those old-fashioned recipes have been passed down and shared with family and friends. Here is a collection of nostalgic desserts that will keep the treasures of yesterday at your fingertips and close to your heart.

quickie cranberry cakes

1/2 cup sugar
1/4 cup water
1 tbsp orange rind, grated
1 cup dried cranberries
1 tbsp rum extract
2 cups all-purpose flour
3 tsps baking powder
1/2 tsp salt
1/2 cup butter
3/4 cup sugar
2 eggs
1 tsp vanilla
3/4 cup milk
frosting (see right)

In saucepan mix together sugar, water, and orange rind. Cook over medium heat until boiling; remove from heat. Add cranberries and rum extract and let stand about 30 minutes. Drain well and reserve syrup. In small bowl sift together flour, baking powder, and salt. Cream together butter and sugar; beat in eggs and vanilla. Alternately add dry ingredients and milk to creamed mixture, blending well after each addition. Fill lined or greased muffin cups halfway. Bake at 350 degrees 20 to 25 minutes. Meanwhile, in saucepan heat reserved cranberry syrup. Remove cupcakes from oven and poke tops with fork or knife. Pour 1/2 teaspoon syrup over each hot cupcake. Cool thoroughly before frosting.

frosting

2 tbsps butter
2 tsps orange rind, grated
1/8 tsp salt
2 cups powdered sugar, sifted
2 tbsps orange juice

To make frosting:
In small mixing bowl cream together butter, orange rind, and salt. Beat in powdered sugar and orange juice alternately; cream well.

makes about 2 dozen

afternoon pineapple cakes

makes about 1 1/2 dozen

2 cups all-purpose flour
1 tsp baking powder
1 tsp salt
1/2 tsp baking soda
1/2 cup sugar
1/2 cup brown sugar, firmly packed
1/2 cup shortening
2 eggs
1/2 cup crushed pineapple (do not drain)
1/2 cup water
1 tsp vanilla
1 cup (6 oz.) semisweet chocolate pieces
frosting (see left)

frosting

2 tbsps butter, melted
1 1/2 cups powdered sugar, sifted and divided
2 tbsps crushed pineapple (do not drain)

To make frosting:
In small mixing bowl beat together butter and 1/2 cup powdered sugar. Mix in pineapple alternately with remaining 1 cup powdered sugar; beat well until spreadable. If necessary, thin with milk.

In small bowl sift together flour, baking powder, salt, and baking soda. Cream together sugar, brown sugar, and shortening. Beat in eggs; beat well after adding each. Stir in pineapple. Alternately add dry ingredients and water to pineapple mixture, blending well after each addition. Mix in vanilla and chocolate pieces. Fill lined or greased muffin cups halfway. Bake at 350 degrees 20 to 25 minutes. Cool thoroughly before frosting.

1/2 cup butter
1/4 cup powdered sugar, sifted
1/2 tsp salt
1 1/2 cups all-purpose flour, sifted
2 tbsps milk
filling (see below)

in mixing bowl cream together butter, powdered sugar, and salt. Gradually add flour and milk. Stir well with fork until dough sticks together. On floured surface roll dough to 1/8-inch thick. Cut 4-inch circles and lay into tart pans or over undersides of muffin cups. Using fork poke generously. Bake at 425 degrees 8 to 10 minutes; cool.

filling

3 egg yolks
1/4 cup orange juice
1 tsp lemon juice
1/2 cup sugar
1/8 tsp salt
1 cup whipping cream
1 tbsp orange rind, grated
orange slices, quartered for garnish

To make filling:
In top of double boiler lightly beat egg yolks. Stirring constantly, gradually add orange juice and lemon juice. Blend in sugar and salt. Stirring constantly, cook over boiling water until thick; cool. In small mixing bowl whip cream until very thick; carefully fold into cooled mixture. Gently stir in orange rind and refrigerate. Divide into tart shells and garnish each with orange slice.

cream-filled orange cakes

makes about 10

apple squares

1 1/2 cups all-purpose flour
1 tsp salt
1/2 cup shortening
1 egg
1/4 cup sour cream
1 tbsp lemon juice
2 cups (3 medium) apples,
    peeled, cored, and chopped
1/4 cup nuts, chopped
1/3 cup sugar
1/4 tsp cinnamon

Grease baking sheet. In medium mixing bowl sift together flour and salt. Using pastry cutter or fork cut in shortening until dough becomes crumbly. Mix together egg, sour cream, and lemon juice. Add to flour mixture and stir until dough sticks together. On floured surface roll half of dough into rectangle the size of baking sheet. Carefully lay pastry onto baking sheet. In small bowl mix together apples, nuts, sugar, and cinnamon; pour evenly over pastry, leaving small rim of pastry visible. Roll other half of dough to same size. Dampen edges of bottom pastry and carefully lay second pastry over top; press edges together to seal. Fold edges up to form lip to keep juices from escaping. Using knife cut slits to mark 16 individual serving squares. Bake at 375 degrees 40 to 45 minutes.

makes 16 servings

island dessert

1 cup plus 3 tbsps all-purpose flour, divided
1 1/2 tsps baking powder
1/2 tsp salt
1/3 cup plus 3 tbsps sugar, divided
1/4 cup shortening
1 egg, beaten
1 tsp vanilla
1/3 cup milk
1/2 cup jam, any flavor
1/2 tsp cinnamon
2 tbsps butter, melted
whipped cream, for garnish

grease and flour bottom of 8 x 8 x 2-inch pan. In small bowl sift together 1 cup flour, baking powder, and salt. Cream together 1/3 cup sugar and shortening. Beat in egg and vanilla. Alternately add dry ingredients and milk, blending well after each addition. Pour into pan; spread jam over top. Blend together remaining 3 tablespoons flour, remaining 3 tablespoons sugar, cinnamon, and butter. Sprinkle evenly over jam and bake at 350 degrees 25 to 30 minutes. Serve warm with whipped cream.

makes 8 servings

dutch oven apple cake

3 tbsps butter

1 1/3 cups brown sugar, firmly packed

2 cups (3 medium) apples, peeled, cored, and
thinly sliced

1/3 cup raisins

1 1/3 cups all-purpose flour

2 tsps baking powder

1/2 tsp salt

1/4 cup sugar

1/3 cup shortening

2 eggs, separated (reserve whites)

1 tsp vanilla

2/3 cup milk

In dutch oven melt butter; remove from heat. Sprinkle 2/3 cup brown sugar into melted butter. Lay apple slices in bottom and sprinkle raisins on top. In small mixing bowl sift together flour, baking powder, and salt. Cream together sugar, remaining 2/3 cup brown sugar, and shortening. Beat in egg yolks and vanilla. Alternately add milk and dry ingredients to creamed mixture; mix well after each addition. In small mixing bowl beat egg whites until stiff and still moist. Gently fold into batter and pour over apples and raisins. Bake at 350 degrees 35 to 45 minutes. Remove from dutch oven immediately.

gingerbread

2 cups all-purpose flour
1 1/4 cups sugar
1 tbsp cinnamon
1 tsp baking powder
1 1/2 tsps ginger
1/4 tsp salt
1/2 cup shortening
1 egg
2 tbsps molasses
1 tsp baking soda
1 cup buttermilk
1 tbsp butter

grease and flour bottom of 12 x 8 x 2-inch pan. In large mixing bowl sift together flour, sugar, cinnamon, baking powder, ginger, and salt. Using pastry cutter or fork cut in shortening until mixture is crumbly. Measure 1/2 cup crumb mixture and set aside. To remaining crumb mixture mix in egg, molasses, baking soda, and buttermilk. Beat about 1 to 2 minutes. Pour into pan. Using fork cut butter into reserved crumb mixture until well blended and sprinkle over batter. Bake at 350 degrees 30 to 35 minutes.

Make All Your Desserts Sensational

makes 1 cake

blueberry crumble cake

cups all-purpose flour
1/2 cups sugar
/3 cup butter
tsps baking powder
tsp salt
eggs, separated
(reserve whites)
cup milk
cup blueberries, fresh,
frozen, or canned, drained
whipped cream, for garnish

imagine...

makes 1 cake

grease and flour bottom of 12 x 8 x 2-inch rectangle pan. In large mixing bowl sift together flour and sugar. Using pastry cutter or fork cut in butter until mixture becomes crumbly. Measure 3/4 cup flour mixture and set aside. To remaining flour mixture beat in baking powder, salt, egg yolks, and milk; beat about 2 minutes. In small mixing bowl beat egg whites until stiff and still moist. Gently fold into batter and pour into pan. Spread blueberries over batter and sprinkle reserved crumb mixture over top. Bake at 350 degrees 40 to 50 minutes. Top with whipped cream before serving.

baked strawberry dessert

1 pkg (1 pound) frozen strawberries, thawed
2 cups all-purpose flour
1 1/4 cups sugar
1 tsp baking soda
1/2 tsp salt
1/2 cup shortening
1/2 cup sour cream
3 eggs
1 tsp vanilla
whipped cream, for garnish

grease and flour bottom of 12 x 8 x 2-inch rectangle pan. Drain berries and reserve juice. In large mixing bowl sift together flour, sugar, baking soda, and salt. Beat in shortening, sour cream, eggs, and vanilla; beat at least 2 minutes. Gently fold in strawberries and pour into pan. Bake at 350 degrees 35 to 45 minutes. Top with whipped cream and reserved strawberry juice.

DOESN'T FALL APART...EVEN WITH SHORTCAKE

makes 1 cake

Strawberry Dessert!

northwest cranberry cobbler

2 1/4 cups all-purpose flour
1/3 cup plus 2 tbsps sugar, divided
2 tsps baking powder
1/2 tsp salt
1/4 cup plus 2 tbsps butter
1 cup milk
2 cups (1-pound can) cranberry sauce
1/4 tsp cinnamon

In large mixing bowl sift together flour, 1/3 cup sugar, baking powder, and salt. Melt 2 tbsps butter and mix into milk. Stir into dry ingredients; mix well. In saucepan heat cranberry sauce. Melt remaining 1/4 cup butter in 2-quart casserole. Pour half of batter in casserole; carefully pour hot cranberry sauce over batter. Using spoon drop remaining batter onto cranberry sauce. Blend remaining 2 tbsps sugar and cinnamon and sprinkle over cobbler. Bake at 350 degrees 35 to 40 minutes.

makes 8 servings

apple ginger cake

2 cups all-purpose flour
1 tsp baking powder
1 tsp salt
1/2 tsp baking soda
1 1/2 tsps ginger
1 tsp cinnamon
1/2 cup shortening
2/3 cup boiling water
1 egg
1/2 cup sugar
1/2 cup molasses
topping (see right)

grease and flour bottom of 8 x 8 x 2-inch pan. In small bowl sift together flour, baking powder, salt, baking soda, ginger, and cinnamon; set aside. Melt shortening in boiling water. Add egg and sugar, beating well until thick. Stir in molasses; add dry ingredients and beat well. Pour batter into pan and bake at 350 degrees 35 to 45 minutes. Serve warm with topping.

topping

1 cup whipping cream
1/2 cup powdered sugar, sifted
2 tbsps lemon juice
1 cup sweetened applesauce

To make topping:
In small mixing bowl beat whipping cream until thick. Carefully fold in rest of ingredients and chill.

makes 1 cake

raspberry cake dessert

1/2 cup butter
1 cup sugar
1 egg
1/4 cup milk
1 tsp vanilla
1/2 tsp salt
1 1/4 cups all-purpose flour, sifted
1/4 cup blanched almonds, toasted
    and chopped
whipped cream
butter filling (see right)
raspberry filling (see right)

butter filling

1/2 cup butter
1 1/2 cups powdered sugar, sifted
1 egg

To make butter filling:
In small mixing bowl cream together butter and powdered sugar. Beat in egg until fluffy.

raspberry filling

1/4 cup sugar
2 tbsps cornstarch
1 10-oz. pkg frozen red raspberries

To make raspberry filling:
In saucepan mix together sugar and cornstarch. Stirring constantly, add raspberries and cook until thick. Cool completely.

makes 1 cake

grease and flour bottom of 8 x 8 x 2-inch pan. In medium mixing bowl cream together butter and sugar. Beat in egg, milk, vanilla, and salt. Stir in flour and almonds. Pour batter into pan and bake at 350 degrees 30 to 35 minutes. Remove from pan and cool. Using sharp knife cut cake in half horizontally to make two layers. Spread bottom layer with butter filling, then raspberry filling. Top with second layer and spread whipped cream on top and sides. Refrigerate at least 4 hours before serving.

fresh apple pastry

1 1/3 cups plus 1 tbsp all-purpose flour, divided
1/2 tsp salt
1/2 cup butter
4 to 5 tbsps cold water
1 cup (1 medium) apple, peeled, cored, and thinly sliced
3 tbsps sugar, divided
2 tbsps slivered almonds

In small mixing bowl sift together 1 1/3 cups flour and salt. Using pastry cutter or fork cut in butter until mixture is crumbly. Sprinkle water over mixture and stir until dough sticks together. On floured surface roll dough into 12-inch square. Gently lay dough on ungreased baking sheet. Mix together remaining 1 tbsp flour and apple slices. Sprinkle 2 tablespoons sugar onto apple mixture and gently stir. Spread apple slices down center third of dough. Fold over each end 1/2 inch. Fold each side over apple mixture, leaving about 1 inch of apples exposed. Sprinkle remaining 1 tablespoon sugar and almonds over exposed apples. Bake at 450 degrees 15 to 20 minutes.

makes 6 servings

1 1/2 cups flour, sifted
2 tsps baking powder
1 tsp salt
3/4 cup butter
3/4 cup sugar
1 egg
2 tsps vanilla
1 1/2 cups quick-cooking rolled oats
topping (see below)

butterscotch toppers

In small mixing bowl stir together flour, baking powder, and salt. Cream together butter and sugar. Beat in egg and vanilla. Fold in oats and dry ingredients; mix well. Refrigerate 1 hour. On floured surface roll half of dough until 1/8-inch thick. Using 2 1/2-inch round cutter, cut dough into rounds and place on ungreased baking sheet. Form topping into 1/2-inch balls and place in middle of each round. Bake at 350 degrees 10 to 12 minutes.

topping

1 cup (6 oz.) butterscotch pieces
2 tbsps butter
1/2 cup sugar
1 egg
2 tbsps flour
1 cup flaked coconut

makes 1 1/2 dozen

To make topping:
In small saucepan melt butterscotch pieces and butter over low heat. Remove and stir in sugar, egg, flour, and coconut; mix well.

country peach bake

serves 9

9rease 8 x 8 x 2-inch pan. In small mixing bowl sift together flour, baking soda, salt, cinnamon, and nutmeg. Cream together butter, lemon rind, lemon juice, and brown sugar. Add cornflakes and dry ingredients until mixture becomes crumbly. Press half of mixture into bottom of pan. Cut-side down, arrange peach halves on top. Sprinkle remaining mixture over top and bake at 350 degrees 45 to 50 minutes. Serve warm with whipped cream.

1 cup all-purpose flour
1/2 tsp baking soda
1/2 tsp salt
1/2 tsp cinnamon
1/4 tsp nutmeg
1/2 cup butter
1 tsp lemon rind, grated
1 tsp lemon juice
1/2 cup brown sugar, firmly packed
1/2 cup cornflakes, crushed
9 peach halves, fresh or canned, well drained
whipped cream, for garnish

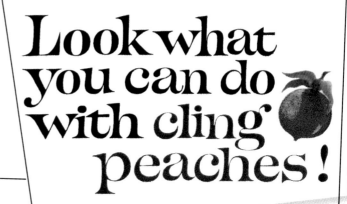

Look what you can do with cling peaches!

WHY didn't
I try this
BEFORE?

index

other desserts